The Mountain of Blessing

The Mountain of Blessing

Exploring the Beatitudes

Rob Marshall

First published in 2026 by Canterbury Press

Editorial office
3rd Floor, Invicta House
110 Golden Lane,
London EC1Y 0TG, UK
www.canterburypress.co.uk

Canterbury Press is an imprint of Hymns Ancient & Modern Ltd
(a registered charity)

HYMNS Ancient & Modern

Hymns Ancient & Modern® is a registered trademark of
Hymns Ancient & Modern Ltd
13A Hellesdon Park Road, Norwich,
Norfolk NR6 5DR, UK

British Library Cataloguing in Publication data

A catalogue record for this book is available
from the British Library

ISBN: 978-1-78622-637-2

EU GPSR Authorized Representative
LOGOS EUROPE, 9 rue Nicolas Poussin, 17000, LA ROCHELLE, France
E-mail: Contact@logoseurope.eu

Typeset by Regent Typesetting

Contents

The Beatitudes

Blessed are the poor in spirit,
for theirs is the kingdom of heaven.

Blessed are those who mourn,
for they will be comforted.

Blessed are the meek,
for they will inherit the earth.

Blessed are those who hunger and thirst for righteousness,
for they will be filled.

Blessed are the merciful,
for they will be shown mercy.

Blessed are the pure in heart,
for they will see God.

Blessed are the peacemakers,
for they will be called children of God.

Blessed are those who are persecuted because of righteousness
for theirs is the kingdom of heaven.

Matthew 5.3–10

PART ONE

Background

Preface

What does it mean to be genuinely happy? It is a question that Jesus seems to be asking in the Beatitudes. It is as appropriate a question in today's disjointed and complex world as it was in his own time. But as Jesus announces the arrival of a dynamic new way of living, which he calls the kingdom, a new way to happiness is pointed out to all believers.

When we live the Beatitudes, we become signs of the kingdom – not in grand gestures, but in small, faithful acts: choosing gentleness over retaliation, listening before judging, forgiving when it is costly, standing beside the vulnerable, speaking truth with love.

The Beatitudes are not ideals for the few: they are the calling of every Christian. They are the shape of a life patterned after Jesus himself. And when we live them, we discover that the blessing promised at the beginning and the end of these sayings is already here. Jesus lays out the challenge of faith simply and unequivocally. He leaves his disciples – and us – in no doubt about the life to which we are called.

Of all the pilgrim sites along the shores of the Sea of Galilee associated with Jesus' ministry, few are as beautiful and evocative as the place traditionally linked to his Sermon on the Mount (Matthew 5—7), during which he spoke the Beatitudes.

The Church of the Beatitudes is a place I have visited many times with pilgrims from across the world. But I wrote this book against the backdrop of a deeply painful conflict between Israel and the people of Gaza that has, at times, spread to the West Bank and further across Israel's borders. During this time, the beautiful Church of the Beatitudes, along with many other major pilgrimage sites, was significantly affected by the unrest – a reminder that sacred places, so central to the emergence of the Christian faith, exist within a land marked by deep tensions and human suffering.

As the setting for what are perhaps Jesus' most well-known sayings, the Church of the Beatitudes emphasizes how clearly the message of these words is as relevant today as it was in the first century.

There are two versions of the Beatitudes in the Gospels. The better known is in the Gospel of Matthew (5.1–12) while the other is in Luke's Gospel (6.17–26). Both versions deal with the heart of Jesus' kingdom teaching, but there are notable differences between them. In Matthew, Jesus addresses his disciples on a mountain (perhaps Matthew wants us to understand Jesus as the new Moses), whereas, in Luke, Jesus speaks to a large crowd on the plain. Matthew's Beatitudes consist of eight blessings where Luke's version has four blessings and four corresponding woes.

Matthew's Beatitudes are more spiritual in tone, forming part of the larger sermon. By contrast, Luke's version – often referred to as the Sermon on the Plain – places a stronger emphasis on social justice, consistent with the wider themes of his Gospel. For example, where Matthew speaks of the 'poor in spirit' (5.3), Luke simply refers to 'the poor' (6.20). Likewise, Matthew's 'those who hunger and thirst for righteousness' (5.6) becomes, in Luke, simply 'those who are hungry' (6.21).

It is hard to overestimate the importance of the wider religious context in which Jesus delivered these sayings. In the Judaism of Jesus' day, there was disagreement with regards to the proper interpretation of the law. There were many different sects, each with their own interpretation as to how the law should be applied and lived out. These various groups appear often in all four Gospels when Jesus' teaching and his miracles and signs are placed under scrutiny. Chief among them are, of course, the Pharisees, the Scribes, the Sadducees and the Essenes.

There were clear expectations of how the laws of the Temple would be upheld, with regards to who could speak to whom, what could or could not happen on the sabbath, or who had the authority to speak about the things of God. It is clear that in each of Matthew's eight Beatitudes, Jesus is challenging outright the religious leaders of his day.

How could this young man from Nazareth claim such authority? The Gospels record that Jesus' wisdom often amazed his hearers; but what was the source of his wisdom? Time and again, against a wider backdrop of Roman occupation, Jesus treads a tightrope between announcing the good news of what he calls the kingdom, while inevitably upsetting the religious authorities. This often results in his exhibiting extreme caution. It ultimately leads to his arrest and execution; but this, according to Jesus' own predictions of his earthly demise, seems always to have been part of a plan.

This book contains an introduction to each of the eight Beatitudes, all including four short reflections on contemporary life and living for the Christian today. I wanted the Beatitudes to be earthed in the challenging, changing and technological world where most of us have to live. There is also a suggested prayer, hymn and painting to enjoy (easily found online, when technology is available). The book can be used at any time of the year, whether by an individual or a number of people. Each section ends with a few simple questions for personal reflection or group discussion.

Between AD 393 and 396, St Augustine of Hippo wrote a profoundly illuminating commentary on the Sermon on the Mount, titled *De Sermone Domini in Monte*. In Book One, he offers a remarkable insight into how the Beatitudes had already begun to settle into the theological consciousness of the Church. We return to St Augustine often as we examine the sayings. A glorious vision of the kingdom is presented here – a kingdom that turns the values of the world upside down and opens up an invitation to a new way of seeing and living.

Even now, my mind goes back to the image of the Church of the Beatitudes, above the waters of the Sea of Galilee. The place speaks of humility and dignity as well as of peace and hope. In the midst of today's conflict and tension, the church and its message stand as a quiet unassuming witness to an alternative way of living set out by Jesus in these sayings.

Revisiting the mountain of blessing, even in troubled times for the Middle East, is the best possible way to start.

Rob Marshall
Hertfordshire, United Kingdom, 2026

Introduction

The setting

Most Holy Land pilgrimages begin at Ben Gurion Airport, just outside Tel Aviv. From here, pilgrims travel either north to Galilee – a journey of around two hours – or south to Jerusalem, which takes just over an hour.

From a chronological perspective, it makes good sense to begin in the Galilee region, where Jesus' ministry began. Many pilgrims find the peace and tranquillity of Galilee a welcome contrast to the noise, hustle and bustle of Jerusalem. In fact, those returning for a second Holy Land pilgrimage often ask to end their journey in Galilee. They are attracted to the still, small voice of calm – associated with the sea where Jesus spent so much of his time.

Although often called the Sea of Galilee, it is, in fact, a freshwater lake. It is around 700 feet below sea level and has an average depth of about 84 feet. It stretches approximately 13 miles from north to south, and just seven miles across at its widest point. Its waters are fed by snowmelt from the mountains to the north, while the valley itself receives little rainfall. Its distinctive shape is easy to recognize on any map of the Holy Land.

It is still possible to see fisherfolk at work around the lake, casting their nets from boats as they did in Jesus' time. Much of the modern-day economy around the lake bordering Tiberias is dependent on pilgrim boat rides, meals and hospitality.

The best view of the Church of the Beatitudes is from the vantage point of a boat. From here, pilgrims can more easily appreciate why Jesus may have chosen this location for his famous Sermon on the Mount overlooking the lake. It resembles a natural amphitheatre, nestled in an otherwise rocky and hilly

Credit: Image by Rob Marshall

landscape, where large crowds could easily gather from nearby towns and villages.

In the Bible, a mountain is often portrayed as a place of divine revelation – where God meets humanity in profound and transformative ways. A comparison is frequently made between Jesus, and his act of sitting down on the mountain to teach the Sermon on the Mount, and Moses, who ascended Mount Sinai to receive the Ten Commandments. Here, Jesus is seen inaugurating a new covenant and offering a new commandment to his followers (see Hebrews 3.3), something Pope Benedict XVI sees as the 'new Ten Commandments' and part of the essential Jewish backdrop to our understanding.[1]

As pilgrim boats bob up and down on the Sea of Galilee, their passengers are encouraged to imagine the scene. The evocative words of the American Quaker John Greenleaf Whittier's much loved hymn 'Dear Lord and Father of Mankind' is often sung by English-speaking groups. While on these boats, I have often gazed across at the wider scenery and tried to imagine what it

1 See Pope Benedict XVI, *Jesus of Nazareth: From the Baptism in the Jordan to the Transfiguration* (Bloomsbury, 2008).

looked like in Jesus' day. Undoubtedly, very little has changed. Bananas, dates and cotton are still grown in the surrounding fields. The views of the mountains and hills remain the same.

Turning off a winding mountain road, littered with centuries-old volcanic basalt rock, a coach eventually arrives at the Church of the Beatitudes.

There is a 'security' entrance gate with a barrier, a large coach and car park, a kiosk selling refreshments, an upmarket gift shop, the church itself and a guest house hosting pilgrims.

The octagonal Church of the Beatitudes is modest in size. Designed by the renowned Italian architect Antonio Barluzzi, it was built in the 1930s on the remains of a fourth-century Byzantine church. Each of the eight sides of the church represents one of Jesus' blessed sayings. Because of its small interior, the church is best suited for individuals or smaller groups. To accommodate larger gatherings, the site features numerous outdoor altars, many of them with canopies providing shade for pilgrims and worshippers as they pray and celebrate. In better times, groups of all sizes arrive daily to remember Jesus' Sermon on the Mount. Priests and ministers, from many countries and representing many nationalities and denominations, lead their people in prayer and worship.

Credit: Image used courtesy of Telesphora Pavlou

The site is cared for by the Franciscan Missionary Sisters of the Immaculate Heart of Mary, who offer hospitality and run the guest house.

Priests dressed in an array of vestments carry small baskets from the vestry. These are provided by the sisters and contain communion sets, crosses, candles and offertory baskets. The generosity of faithful pilgrims has helped sustain these holy sites.

Pilgrims traditionally worship in every corner of this gorgeous pilgrim place. The Bible is read; prayers are offered; forgiveness is asked for. The peace is shared. Mass is celebrated, and beautiful spiritual songs in many languages – *abencoada*, *siunattu*, *beni*, *adlott*: 'blessed' – echo around the various chapels with the sound of nature as a backdrop. Worship continues throughout the whole day and overlaps from group to group as pilgrims recount again and again the Beatitudes.

But, with the Golan Heights nearby and the Syrian capital Damascus a mere 40 miles away, every so often a military aircraft or sonic boom will break the peace. At some point on most days, there is a noise associated with a lack of peace, a reminder of the sinfulness of humanity.

So, this is the unique and glorious holy place of the Sermon on the Mount and the Beatitudes. In Jesus' day, people would have flocked from the many villages when news broke of this new teacher from Nazareth. What was this kingdom he was talking about? They wanted to know more.

Now take some time out to imagine yourself in this place of peace and wonder: pray and ask what Jesus wants to say to you today through these eight remarkable and enduring sayings as our time of exploration begins.

Jesus the teacher

> When Jesus saw the crowds, he went up on a mountainside and sat down. His disciples came to him, and he began to teach them. (Matthew 5.1–2)

Of the many possible descriptions that could sum up Jesus' work, 'teacher' is one of the most obvious and common. From the start of his public ministry, after many years of preparation, Jesus' chief calling is, it seems, to teach.

Jesus the teacher is clear about his specialist subject: the kingdom. When he taught, it seems the people listened. He calls disciples specifically to help him in this task. He teaches them as the Twelve, alongside groups and crowds of various sizes. He sometimes teaches directly. At other times, he uses stories (parables) about seeds, birds, fishing, baking bread, and other everyday sights and sounds to relate his message to the everyday lives of his hearers.

Having worked in many schools, I find it a joy to witness so many different styles of teaching. Every teacher is unique. Each year for the past decade, our parish has organized a 'welcome breakfast' for newly qualified teachers starting their careers in local schools. These gatherings are always uplifting when you consider the diversity of those responding to a call to teach. It takes all sorts of people to be good teachers and to share the cumulative wisdom of knowledge and experience.

In his 1983 book, *The Teaching of Jesus*, the New Testament scholar Norman Anderson observed that Jesus' teaching stands as an 'Everest alone', towering in its clarity, depth and originality. Jesus' relaxed and extemporaneous style seemed new and strikingly different.

Whether conversing with a Samaritan woman (as he should not have done, given the strict social customs of the day; John 4.9ff.), instructing his disciples (Matthew 28.19–20) or addressing the crowds (Matthew 13.2, where a gathering is so large that he is forced to teach from a boat), Jesus is clear and compelling. His words resonate with a kind of authority the people had not encountered before. His use of parables (of which there are many) and sayings (such as the Beatitudes) sometimes serves to hide any 'true' meaning, for reasons we will go on to explore.

It can take quite some time for a new Christian to realize that the Bible as we know it did not just appear in the form we have today. For instance, there was a gap of at least several decades between Jesus' actual teaching and his words being written down. So, what is known as 'oral tradition' reflects a period during which the first Christian communities memorized and passed on the key sayings of Jesus by word of mouth. In terms of communication, they were vastly different days from ours. The Jewish practice of oral memorization and communal recitation, with which Jesus would have been well acquainted, was popular and remains so today.

Matthew's unique take

The context of Matthew's Gospel, as the source of the Beatitudes we are exploring, is important.

Matthew has been widely accepted as the 'Jewish' Gospel. Its author seems intent on painting a portrait of Jesus as the fulfiller of the Law and the Prophets and as the long-awaited Messiah. The Gospel of Matthew has a unique structure. As well as quoting the Hebrew Scriptures widely, there is also a significant amount of exclusive material that is in none of the other Gospels – most noticeably the well-known birth stories of Jesus concerning Joseph and the visit of the Magi.

Matthew also uses the term 'kingdom of heaven' rather than the 'kingdom of God' (as is usual in Luke and Mark). Whether or not this difference in Matthew means anything more than an alternative term for the same thing, we will consider in a moment.

It is within this context of the Gospel of Matthew that the Beatitudes serve as kingdom sayings – declarations that unveil a whole new order. Here is a world where the poor in spirit, the meek, the merciful and the peacemakers are honoured as true citizens of God's world: those travelling as pilgrims on a road to lasting peace and happiness, leading ultimately to salvation.

Good news of the kingdom

The Beatitudes reflect the values and priorities of the kingdom. They are what might be called today its vision statement. More than just moral principles, they serve as a blueprint for discipleship, guiding followers of Jesus in how to live out the kingdom in everyday life.

My own understanding – and indeed, my lasting excitement – about the kingdom in Jesus' teaching was profoundly shaped as a teenager while reading biblical studies at Sheffield University.

Bruce Chilton, a young American New Testament scholar, was my tutor. In a similar way to those teachers, mentioned on p. 11, who leave an impression, Bruce planted a seed about the importance of the kingdom that has forever stayed with me. Over the decades, he has continued to write extensively on the subject of Jesus and the kingdom, and is often quoted as saying, 'In all Jesus' teachings, no single concept is more important, more central, more resonant than the Kingdom of God. The Kingdom of God figures as a vital concept within the Scriptures of Israel.'[2]

The way in which Jesus presents this 'kingdom' from the very start, and consequently throughout his ministry, poses lots of questions. The kingdom is at hand, but not yet here. It is best understood in worldly terms but speaks mainly of heaven and future glory. Through the stories Jesus tells, the kingdom represents the opposite of what the religious leaders of his day were articulating as the true way to godliness and peace.

Instead of their legalistic jargon, Jesus' focus is on love in action.

A teacher knows that their success in transmitting what they want their students to learn is down to a variety of factors. Assessing whether the wisdom has been received at the end of the lesson is part of what being a good teacher is all about. In order to achieve maximum impact, Jesus keeps it simple. At the same time, he presents the kingdom with a degree of profundity that is still shrouded in mystery as the jigsaw pieces come together.

---

2 Quoted in Matthew Fox, 'The Kingdom of God Is US – Each and All!', *Patheos*, 9 August 2013.

The idea of a kingdom comes first in Mark's Gospel where Jesus declares: 'The time has come, the kingdom of God has come near. Repent and believe the good news!' (Mark 1.15). It is introduced boldly and without hesitation immediately after Jesus' baptism.

Jesus turns to the crowd – already, it would seem, captivated by his presence – and declares that the kingdom is not a distant hope, but something near, 'at hand', breaking into their present reality. This is also the essence of what Mark describes as the *euangelion*, the 'good news' with which he opens his Gospel. This 'good news' is for everyone. Regardless of religion, background, faith tradition or social status, all are invited to share in the kingdom – on the condition that they repent, turn around and begin again.

The kingdom and the 'good news' are linked. The arrival of the kingdom is the 'good news'; it is an invitation into life under God's reign. Together, they form the foundation of Jesus' entire teaching. Both Luke and Matthew have more references to the kingdom than Mark. Like Mark, Luke uses the phrase 'kingdom of God' rather than Matthew's 'kingdom of heaven'. In Luke, there is a more Gentile feel to the kingdom than in Matthew. The kingdom of heaven in Matthew starts with a sense of fulfilment of the Jewish expectation concerning a future Messiah, whereas the kingdom of God in Luke is more universal.

It is indeed because of this that Matthew portrays Jesus as the fulfiller of the hopes of Israel and the bringer-in of a new kingdom order. So, by Jesus' sheer presence, the kingdom is at hand. Jesus does not just announce the kingdom – he embodies it. In him, the reign of God has drawn closer, and this is part of the crucial context in which Matthew presents the Sermon on the Mount.

As the kingdom jigsaw puzzle began to form in the minds of those who heard the teaching of Jesus, the early apostles grew more confident about explaining the kingdom and its values.

As he travelled widely, St Paul explained in his letter to the Romans that the values of this kingdom – recharged by the Holy Spirit of Pentecost – are now what transforms the heart: 'The kingdom of God is not a matter of eating and drinking, but of righteousness, peace and joy in the Holy Spirit' (Romans 14.17).

These are the hallmarks of the kingdom life – a life rooted in God's grace, open to all who are willing to step into its light.

Blessed

I have noticed that many young people today use the word 'bless' as a way of expressing delight or happiness in response to good news or a 'nice moment'. The word seems to have replaced exclamations like 'Oh great!' or 'How lovely!' It has become a gentle and heartfelt reaction that captures something emotionally significant.

The Greek word translated 'blessed' in English is *makarioi.* It can simply mean 'happy' or 'fortunate' but also carries a deeper meaning, which is why 'blessed' is more often used in the biblical translation of Jesus' sayings on the Mount of Beatitudes. *Makarioi* speaks not just of a passing emotion, but of a state of being in harmony with God's kingdom – a kind of inner flourishing, rooted in grace, even in unexpected circumstances. It is a reminder that true blessedness may not always look like worldly success; instead, it is aligned with values such as humility, mercy and peace, which sums up the overall thrust of the Beatitudes.

Jesus would have been aware of these kinds of words through his knowledge of the Hebrew Bible. In the Psalms, the Hebrew word for blessed is *ashrei*, and when Jesus used the word here, translated for us in Matthew 5, the Hebrew equivalent may well have been in his mind.

> Blessed is the one who does not walk in step with the wicked. (Psalm 1.1)

> Blessed is the one whose transgressions are forgiven. (Psalm 32.1)

> Blessed is the nation whose God is the LORD. (Psalm 33.12)

> Blessed are all who fear the LORD, who walk in obedience to him. (Psalm 128.1)

To be blessed in this sense is to experience God's presence and vindication even in times of trouble and uncertainty.

I think how often Christians in the most awful of situations may have found real comfort in the experience of those who lived before them. Their example speaks to them from one generation to another. Hebrew wisdom describes life itself as a blessing. God's desire is to bless the people if they adhere to the covenant, to see them live in joy and peace. A recurring challenge is human sinfulness, standing in the way of such flourishing. The battle between good and evil is never far from the surface throughout Scripture, and Jesus here faces it head on.

So *ashrei* and *makarioi* convey the idea of being blessed. Both define a state of happiness and a sense of flourishing in faith because of a deep understanding of God and the values we should embrace and uphold.

In the Beatitudes, Jesus proclaims the kingdom by turning the traditional understanding of what real blessing is on its head. He presents a radical vision: those who are usually overlooked or dismissed – the poor in spirit, the mourners, the meek, and so on – are declared by Jesus as truly blessed.

As we explore each of the Beatitudes in turn, we keep all of this in mind: these are not just lofty ideals or poetic sayings. They are invitations to a new way of life, as God intended us to be. Bishop Steve Croft, in his stimulating guide *Pilgrim Journeys: The Beatitudes – 40 Days of Reflections*, suggests, 'Each quality is set within a blessing. Each blessing is set within a promise. These are words of hope and joy.'

We now explore each of them in the context of our lives and the world we are called to live in today.

PART TWO

Reflections

1

Humility

Blessed are the poor in spirit,
for theirs is the kingdom of heaven.

> Jesus here reminds us that it is not what we have that matters but what we are, at the centre of ourselves: inwardly poor, with a heart empty of cares, free from consumerism and obsession with past and future; but open to the coming of God's kingdom, which fills our poverty with divine richness.
> (Dr Earl Collins, Canon Chancellor of Chichester Cathedral)

Humility may not be in fashion today, but it would seem to be high on Jesus' agenda. This first Beatitude, addressing the poor in spirit, confirms that it is to them that the kingdom belongs. It is an overture to the rest of the sayings.

The disciples would not immediately have understood what Jesus was saying. On one level, the message is clear and simple. But on another, as is the case with all eight Beatitudes, some thought and reflection are needed. The true ramifications of a poverty of spirit leading to an understanding of the kingdom would have taken some working out by the disciples.

St Augustine of Hippo regards the eight Beatitudes as a spiritual crescendo. Each builds on the last, forming a connected flow of spiritual guidance. Jesus' immediate focus is on humility, the foundation stone of all Christian virtues, as Augustine points out: 'Whoever is puffed up is not poor in spirit.' The starting point for any Christian on their pilgrim journey, then, is the recognition that they need to empty themselves of what they know to be wrong in their lives, in order to embrace the values of the kingdom.

Pope Benedict XVI made frequent references to the Beatitudes. Israel's experience of exile was important, he believed, to understand this Beatitude fully. Stripped of a homeland and identity, having seemingly lost everything, Israel came to realize – often painfully – that it was in moments of profound poverty and dependence that they drew closest to God. In losing what they had always taken for granted, they discovered a deeper truth: that God is near to the broken-hearted and that spiritual transformation, from perceived poverty to riches, often comes out of the worst of times.

The relationship between each of the Beatitudes and Jesus' teaching in general is realized at different stages by his audiences. First, the disciples hear the words fresh from Jesus' lips. Then, as his ministry develops and as the full extent of all he will endure unfolds, what he said or did previously is revised and reinterpreted. This is not only because Jesus did not want or expect his hearers to know the answers right away. It is also because the magnitude of the implications of the kingdom, now at hand, was going to take some time to be absorbed and understood.

It is only with hindsight that we understand how the theme of this first Beatitude undergirds much of Jesus' other teaching and ministry. Jesus came not to be served but to serve (Mark 10.45) and, in so doing, the Son of Man was to give his life as a ransom for many.

After the resurrection, and with the Early Church doing its work in the face of many hurdles that it needed to overcome, the realization of the extent of Jesus' own humility became clearer and more celebrated.

Writing to the Philippians, Paul asserts that Jesus 'humbled himself and became obedient to death – even death on a cross' (2.8). Based on his example, the call to humility, taking up one's own cross and following Jesus, is the true calling for anyone wanting to follow the path of discipleship.

This also applies to the whole Church. Reassessing its priorities in mission, and the best use of its various resources in a quest for humility, is a huge undertaking, especially in recent times when the Church has faced many internal issues.

My dear friend Earl Collins, now a Residentiary Canon at Chichester, stresses above all that it is not what we have that matters, but what we are, at the centre of ourselves: 'inwardly poor, with a heart empty of cares, free from consumerism and obsession with past and future, but open to the coming of God's kingdom, which fills our poverty with divine richness'.

How to begin that Christian journey and maintain an element of resilience in an often-hostile world is the beginning and the end of the calling of any Christian today.

Baptism

The Beatitudes present, in poetic form, the priorities of the baptism life. Whether you are preparing for baptism, have recently been baptized, or were baptized many years ago and regularly renew your baptism promises in a church, these blessed sayings speak of both the expectation and the experience of being baptized.

Baptism is one of those experiences that are hard to sum up or to describe. While the actual baptism moment itself is enormously important, it is worth remembering that it is only the start of something. Baptism is relived every day. The promises made are for a lifetime during which God's blessing is asked for daily.

By being prepared to be presented before the gathered church, to confess one's sins, to be anointed by the Holy Spirit and to be washed clean through the waters of baptism, believers inevitably acknowledge how poor in spirit they are in the first place; they can then see clearly the reality of the kingdom life.

One question I am often asked is how babies can be baptized when they are not able to answer for themselves. Most of the baptisms I conduct each year are of children. They are organized by parents and carers to give their young ones (usually babies) a blessing at the start of their lives. The hope of the Church is always that the child will return one day to confirm the promises made at their baptism.

Pause and read these passages and reflect on them: Matthew 3.13–17 or *Mark 1.9–11. Jesus comes to John the Baptist and asks to be baptized.*

There have been various sites around the River Jordan where Christians have, over the centuries, come to re-enact what happened to Jesus. The two best-known sites (because we cannot be sure where it happened) are Yardenit and Qasr al-Yahud. Tradition has it that Jesus came to this general region of the River Jordan to be baptized by John the Baptist. Christians ever since have come to these places to be baptized or to renew their baptism vows.

I have had the honour of leading many baptism vow renewal services at Yardenit. It is a real joy to take a fallen tree branch, dip it in the Jordan and sprinkle the faithful with the holy waters of baptism. It is a great way to remember that, in order to experience the kingdom at work in the world, we must first acknowledge how poor in spirit we are without Jesus. The renewal of baptism vows is frequently one of the central acts of any pilgrimage.

I also enjoy preparing candidates and their families for baptism. They usually make contact voluntarily because they have no church connections. Something prompts new parents to come to church and ask for the sacrament of baptism. It has led to some stimulating conversations.

Preparations are made for the big day. Godparents are chosen as supporters for the newly baptized: they speak on behalf of the children and are called to pray regularly for them. Readings, hymns and poems are also specially chosen.

During the service itself, the font, as the place for baptism, becomes the focus of attention. This is where water is poured and blessed. The faithful come to be symbolically washed clean. The three great symbols used at baptism are oil, water and light: *water* signifies cleansing and new life; *oil* the presence of the Holy Spirit; and *light* from the baptismal candle (often lit from the Paschal candle) represents Christ's presence guiding the life of the newly baptized.

No one knows where life will lead us. There are many twists and turns. The expected and the unexpected both feature as part of the pilgrim journey. Whenever I baptize a child, my prayer is always that, whatever happens in the life of this newly baptized person, God's presence will be real: that they will indeed be blessed.

After each candidate is presented with their baptism candle at the end of the service, they are all encouraged to go out and shine as lights in the world to the glory of God the Father. The kingdom is now there to embrace for the newly baptized and their families. This momentous event in a Christian's life should be a daily remembrance and the promises often joyfully renewed.

Confirmation

While a priest or deacon baptizes, confirmation is conducted by a bishop. It marks the moment when the baptism promises are confirmed by a candidate or by a child's parents and godparents. Traditionally, confirmation is followed by the moment when a believer receives Holy Communion (the bread and wine) for the first time, although in some churches this can happen before confirmation.

The Easter Vigil is one special service in the Church's year that reflects the powerful symbolism of the journey from baptism to communion. It is usually celebrated on Holy Saturday (the night before Easter) by a diocesan bishop in their cathedral church. The lighting of the holy fire symbolizes the end of a wait for Jesus' resurrection. It is then that those wishing to be baptized and/or confirmed are presented to the bishop by priests from across the diocese.

At this, and any service of confirmation, the bishop asks each candidate if they repent of their sins and invites them publicly to declare their faith. As the name of each candidate is read aloud, the bishop prays over them, 'Confirm, O Lord, your servant [Name] with your Holy Spirit.' Now is the moment of realization that the kingdom is theirs. It is to be embraced in a spirit of deep prayerfulness – and of gratitude to have come to this moment. Each is then anointed with the holy oil as a sign of the Holy Spirit's calling and presence.

Seeing people of all ages and backgrounds being confirmed in large numbers as Easter arrives is uplifting. Usually, the newly confirmed (including those who have been baptized at the same time) then receive their first Communion. As they share in the bread and wine as signs and symbols of Jesus' body and blood, they become full members of the body of Christ, which is the Church.

The Eucharist is a sign of Christ's body gathered together. In the one Spirit, the baptized and confirmed have given their allegiance to Christ and rejected all that is evil. They have no doubt realized that, until this moment, their poverty of spirit was real and acute.

This first Beatitude challenges the hearer to respond. Do you not realize that all is not as it seems? That now is the time to respond to God's call through Christ and put faith into action? These are the blessed ones.

For centuries, the sacraments of baptism, confirmation and the Eucharist have revealed to the penitent and faithful that the kingdom is tangible and made real. It is for them to embrace daily.

Resilience

When the celebrated British actor Sir Ian McKellen fell off the stage on to an audience member at the Noel Coward Theatre in London, it caused both him and the person he landed on physical injury, and made big headlines.

Writing afterwards in *The Times*, the medical columnist Dr Mark Porter posed the question: 'What should we all learn from Ian McKellen's dramatic fall?' He was pleased, he said, that McKellen mentioned 'the continuing emotional repercussions as these are common too, particularly anxiety and loss of confidence'. This is where our spiritual state of mind can take a hit in a similar way to our physical bodies' reaction when we face illness or injury.

When confidence is shattered, it takes courage and humility to pick ourselves up and move forward. Sometimes something happens after which life is never quite the same again. It becomes a kind of turning point. When people hit any kind of spiritual turbulence, it can take an age to recognize that something – it is not always clear exactly what – is needed to overcome it before they are able to pick themselves up and move forward confidently.

This is a topic of conversation people often want to talk about in pastoral situations. They frequently say how they somehow managed to 'stay the course' after a challenging period. They only realized after the event that the ability to get through it was not entirely their own; their strength came from somewhere else.

In such situations, we rarely recognize how poor in spirit we are, or have become, as one day leads on to another. We might then suddenly ask, 'How am I coping?' 'Where is God in all of this?' 'Am I really focused on the kingdom at large, or have I withdrawn into myself and, therefore, inadvertently raised my "poverty of spirit" levels?'

This momentous passage from Paul's letter to the Romans is a rallying call for resilience. It is rooted in the understanding that humility is the required starting point to witness God's blessing in action:

> Not only so, but we also glory in our sufferings, because we know that suffering produces perseverance; perseverance, character; and character, hope. And hope does not put us to shame, because God's love has been poured out into our hearts through the Holy Spirit, who has been given to us. (Romans 3.3–5)

This is why this first Beatitude speaks to our times so clearly. Only the poor in heart can be truly blessed and be inheritors of the kingdom. They are the people who recognize the need for perseverance, character and hope in an often frantic and unpredictable world.

Prayer

Recognizing the importance of both personal prayer and praying with others (including leading others in prayer) is one of the basic ways in which the first Beatitude is applied to everyday life on the Christian journey.

Prayer is not something people usually initiate a conversation about. Perhaps because people think it is a very personal thing (which of course it can be), but also because, as part of the wider worship of the Church, prayer is often left to 'the professionals', which should not be the case.

But even the tiniest suggestion that we assess our prayer life in the light of Jesus' first Beatitude might lead to a realization that any poverty of spirit is reflected in the amount of time each day we give over to God in terms of prayer, meditation and reflection.

As a teacher, Jesus had lots of advice to offer on prayer, including not to hold a grudge or make a show, and to be persistent but not to go on for too long. He gives the Lord's Prayer as an example of how to pray (Matthew 6.5–13).

Perhaps this is a good moment to pause and say the Lord's Prayer quietly and to think about the words as you say them.

Recognizing our need to pray – and to persist in personal prayer – is a vital starting point. It helps us to discover the remedies that enable us to perceive the kingdom more clearly, living with a prayerful awareness that God is always beside us, whether we realize it or not.

It is also worth considering the responsibility of leading prayers in worship on behalf of others. Such a ministry is usually described as 'leading the intercessions'. One or several people may be deputed to offer prayers on behalf of the gathered community. They are to pray for key areas such as the world, the Church, the local community, and the sick and dying.

People take this responsibility extremely seriously and approach it in a variety of ways. Different personalities inevitably fashion the style of leading prayer. It is always important to embrace the nub of the first Beatitude here: to focus on the things of God rather than the things that specifically interest you or what you personally believe. Here, you are leading the prayers for all present.

A diocese recently made a few waves after issuing its parishes with an anti-racist toolkit. The aim was to offer advice that those leading public prayer should try to be as diverse and inclusive as possible. The advice was to 'remember the ever-changing cultural backdrop, avoid bias and any sense of privilege at all costs'. So, if you pray, what do you say?

The author of 1 Timothy puts it like this:

> I urge, then, first of all, that petitions, prayers, intercession and thanksgiving be made for all people – for kings and all those in authority, that we may live peaceful and quiet lives in all godliness and holiness. This is good, and pleases God our Saviour, who wants all people to be saved and to come to a knowledge of the truth. (1 Timothy 2.1–4)

An acknowledgement that prayer is important, that we are poor in spirit without it, and that through prayer we may see the kingdom at work is fundamental to any lifelong Christian journey. Jesus had seen enough hypocrisy among the religious leaders in his own day. From now on, poverty of spirit was the starting point for a life of prayer and spiritual blessing.

Praying

This is a perfect pilgrim prayer, underlining our reliance on God's being present daily:

> O God, forasmuch as without you
> we are not able to please you;
> mercifully grant that your Holy Spirit
> may in all things direct and rule our hearts;

through Jesus Christ your Son our Lord,
who is alive and reigns with you,
in the unity of the Holy Spirit,
one God, now and for ever. Amen.
(Trinity 19 Collect, *Common Worship*)

Listening: 'Rejoice, the Lord Is King'

https://www.youtube.com/watch?v=xA0jM77Qers

This is an uplifting hymn, often sung on the Feast of the Ascension and the Feast of Christ the King. One of Charles Wesley's greatest, it associates Jesus directly with the kingdom he presents in the Beatitudes. The kingdom is expressed as being both present and still to come. Jesus has established himself on the right hand of the Father but the kingdom is not yet complete. Jesus has battled with sin and death and paid the ultimate sacrifice, and light now shines in the darkness.

We are to give thanks and to sing of our hope in Jesus, who turns the sinful values of the world upside down.

As Jesus was lifted up on the cross, so we too lift now our hearts and voices. We are indeed blessed – so rejoice!

Rejoice, the Lord is King!
Your Lord and King adore;
Mortals, give thanks and sing,
And triumph evermore:
Lift up your heart, lift up your voice;
Rejoice; again I say, rejoice!
(Charles Wesley, 1744)

Looking

https://www.vangoghmuseum.nl/en/collection/s0149v1962

Vincent van Gogh, Wheatfield with Crows *(1890), oil on canvas, Van Gogh Museum, Amsterdam.*

The first Beatitude calls us to be resilient in shunning the ways of the world and realizing our poverty of spirit. This will be a constant battle – keeping our eyes fixed firmly on the things of God. When it comes to learning to trust in God, I often think of this verse from Matthew 6.26: 'Look at the birds of the air; they do not sow or reap or store away in barns, and yet your heavenly Father feeds them. Are you not much more valuable than they?'

With this verse in mind, during a recent visit to Amsterdam I viewed Vincent Van Gogh's majestic painting *Wheatfield with Crows*. It is one of the artist's final works and evokes a deep sense of restlessness and searching. Its bold colours (yellow, blue, green) depict the fields, hedges and sky. But what draws the eye most are the crows that roam freely from their flight paths down into the field and back up again. They seem scattered, even chaotic.

But even in the chaos, God is present.

Jesus seems to be saying that our work is not in vain. This idea is particularly when we are attempting to work towards building up the kingdom against all the odds and we feel our resilience to the ways of the world is weak. If the birds of the air are fed by the Father, how much more will God care for us? This is where trust and hope meet faith.

When the going gets tough, it is far too easy to doubt and lack resilience to persist in the things of God. But through Jesus, the kingdom is at hand. Now the future can open up hope. Be strong. Be Resilient. Turn the values of the world on their head. And start living.

Questions

1. What do you remember – or what have you been told – about your baptism?
2. In the light of this chapter, how might you deepen your awareness of what it means to be 'poor in spirit'? Why is this considered a blessing?
3. When you encounter turbulence or difficulty in life, which barriers prevent you from turning to God and asking for help?
4. Reflect on your own prayer life. In which ways might it grow or develop further?

2

Comfort

Blessed are those who mourn,
for they will be comforted.

> No one who mourns feels 'blessed'; but Jesus here surprises us with the extraordinary insight that the mourner is close to the heart of creation, and the depths of grief and disappointment are the seedbed of divine renewal.
> (Canon Angela Tilby, writer and broadcaster)

Here is a Beatitude that disarms the disciples just as much as the first one. We note that this Beatitude may be understood in two ways:

- mourning the loss of a loved one: the practical experience of loss;
- mourning through a failure to live out day by day the priorities of the kingdom that Jesus brings.

Taking the second, more hidden meaning first, St Augustine believed that such mourning is the consequence of a realization that things are badly wrong in terms of our choices and priorities. It is a natural follow-on from the humility necessary to understand a poverty of spirit in the first Beatitude. So, when a believer comes before God and says, 'Look, I realize I have got things badly wrong in terms of life's choices, and I am sad about it,' that is what mourning looks like in the face of the emerging kingdom.

At the same time, Jesus inevitably provides a good moment to reflect on the human experience of loss, mourning and bereavement. It would seem that the disciples can better understand the extent of what Jesus is saying about any kind of spiritual difficulties or loss because of the comparison between the two.

Personal bereavement is experienced in a variety of ways. But it usually comes in one of two contexts: either after a valuable but challenging time of preparation for the death of a loved one, where it becomes expected and anticipated, or, in often more dramatic and entirely unexpected circumstances, following a sudden death. In both cases, the experience is different for everyone, but usually hugely challenging.

There is also what might be called mourning by association. This happens either following the death of a famous person or after news of an international event or tragedy in which death features heavily. For example, there have been many high school shootings in the United States recently and we can only imagine the grief and fear of parents and loved ones. Or we see images following a plane crash, or a natural disaster such as an earthquake, which suddenly hits the headlines.

The death of someone well known, such as the late Queen Elizabeth II, can bring many strangers together to experience deep loss. Two days after her death, I still remember travelling to Buckingham Palace and standing amid a sea of flowers brought by people from all over the world. The crowd mourned together. I took my grandson and told him that history would remember this day. I believe the crowd did feel blessed to be mourning together for someone they loved and respected, whose life had been rooted in service.

This Beatitude, then, takes up the universal human experience of loss and links it to our awareness of our failures to live up to the expectations of the Christian life. Jesus is again addressing the state of things as he finds them: how those purporting to be spiritual guides to others seem to have skewed priorities. Choosing between God's way and the way of the world remains challenging. Self-awareness and realization are key to being blessed here.

The kingdom that Jesus points to in these Beatitudes offers a hope that human beings need in order to be able to focus on God. Jesus suggests that there are now just two commandments: to love God completely and to show that love in the way human beings treat one another. In many ways, it could not be more straightforward.

Pause here and reflect on Matthew 22.24–40. This is our task. We have hope, after all, through God's grace. It is a question of priorities.

Priorities

Jesus could not be clearer in the second Beatitude when it comes to keeping our 'to-do' lists up to date.

I love my list of things I know I have to do. I update it all the time. Some people, of course, do this on their electronic devices; but it is surprising how many people still like the good old-fashioned notepad or even those expensive notebooks that have become all the rage in the past decade. There are the important tasks; the 'pending' items that need attention quite soon; and then those things that seem to be on there permanently without ever being actioned.

We have to navigate a way through a never-ending list of choices to be made each day. Some are simple; some not so. It's part of everyday life and I suppose it always has been.

Ordering how to live our lives in the light of those baptism promises that we talked about earlier is not easy. God should be at the centre of our daily lives, but many find that easier said than done. There always seem to be multiple obstacles preventing us from achieving the right balance between Christian living and earthly distractions.

The sense of failure – or mourning (or that more dramatic word 'lament') – kicks in when we look at the 'to-do' list of our Christian life and realize how far we are falling short: not saying our prayers; giving reading the Bible a lower priority than it deserves; finding excuses not to go to church. Most can identify with a feeling of knowing what is right and what ought to be done and yet, for whatever reason, becoming imprisoned by daily routines and seemingly incapable of responding appropriately.

This is a big theme for the early Church Fathers. St John Chrysostom, for instance, preaches passionately about spreading the gospel and caring for the poor. Yet he laments how easily the Church becomes distracted by internal divisions and worldly concerns, making authentic mission difficult.

That, sadly, is still often the case today. The Church finds it so difficult to get its priorities right. In recent years, safeguarding failures have been the cause of much mourning and lamentation. Comfort comes when we face head on what we know to be wrong. But it cannot be achieved without first going through the mourning process and dealing with it honestly.

Technology, and the way lives are lived today more generally, means that there are even more potential distractions. It is hard to switch off. We will look at this in more detail later. In his book *Jesus of Nazareth: From the Baptism in the Jordan to the Transfiguration*, Pope Benedict XVI observed, 'The standards of the world are turned upside down as soon as things are seen in the right perspective, which is to say, in terms of God's values, so different from those of the world.' So the challenge is to keep our priorities and those of the Church in order.

This Beatitude acknowledges that there remains a distance to go before achieving life's goals and making any necessary adaptations. God comforts those who know that they still have some way to go – which, to be honest, is most of us.

Be upbeat. Be positive. Come to the Lord and ask him to be alongside you in your endeavours to do the right thing. If you feel any sadness that life's priorities are skewed, this is possibly a good thing. For you will be comforted.

Lazarus

From spiritual lament for our earthly shortcomings, we move on to another common human experience – mourning the loss of a loved one.

Mourning someone is one of the greatest challenges for people of all faiths and none. It is difficult in a world where people want instant answers and in which we can suddenly be confronted with the temporary nature of life, relationships and daily existence when sudden loss presents itself. There is hope and a glimmer of light; but that cannot detract from the pain that loss nearly always involves.

Because Jesus was a young man, his death would have been far from the disciples' minds when he spoke this Beatitude; but, in the New Testament, the sight of Jesus eventually hanging on the cross must have caused immense suffering for those who loved him and who were left bewildered.

A relatively short time after Jesus had uttered this Beatitude, the death of his friend Lazarus took place.

Spend some time reading the events in John 11 again to re-acquaint yourself with the sheer drama of what happens.

The story of Lazarus remains one of the best known in the Bible. Even today, in popular culture, Lazarus is remembered as the one who defeated death. He is still recalled in media headlines relating to sports people, politicians and celebrities who looked 'dead and buried' but have somehow been reborn and have relaunched themselves.

The story in John's Gospel evolves over several days and there are various references to the friends of Lazarus mourning his passing. If only Jesus had been there, it would not have happened. The moment of the actual raising of Lazarus has huge dramatic quality: 'When he had said this, Jesus called in a loud voice, "Lazarus, come out!" The dead man came out, his hands and feet wrapped with strips of linen, and a cloth around his face' (John 11.43–44).

Nevertheless, the sorrow and sense of loss felt by Lazarus' family and friends are key here. Let us look at the challenges a bereavement brings.

Bereavement

Mourning a loved one takes place in a variety of ways, over different periods of time and on multiple levels.

Life expectancy was much shorter in Jesus' time, and so when Jesus said the word 'mourn' it is almost certain that the disciples would have thought first of their own experiences of bereavement.

I have taken many funerals during my years as a priest. Rites and rituals have changed over time. Many families now opt for a secular celebrant, though I am surprised how often the Lord's Prayer and the odd hymn is slipped in 'just in case'.

Following the death of a loved one, there is usually a dual need at the final goodbye to express a sense of loss and also offer thanksgiving for all that was happy and enduring in a person's life.

I remember being slightly alarmed to hear, on a TV documentary, of a parent saying why they had bought their child a hamster: when the pet died, it would teach the child something about losing someone they loved. I am sure there are better ways – such as talking about it, for instance – but I suppose they had a point.

A key series of questions that I am often asked after someone has died is, 'What happens next? Where is my loved one now? How do I know? What if I cannot quite believe it – is that all right?' So many people who would not say that they are Christians seem to believe in something that resembles heaven, an eternal place of peace and light; but many wrestle with it for the rest of their lives as their own mortality comes into focus.

Christian communities usually pray both for the bereaved and for those who have died, that they may 'rest in peace and rise in glory'. People often tell me how much comfort it brings and the sense of hope they experience. At All Souls, which falls at the beginning of November, churches often invite those whose loved ones' funerals have taken place during past years. The people who come appreciate being able to light a candle, meet with others and share their memories. It is a special time to be together in what is an ongoing process of mourning and remembering.

It is my experience, after four decades of ministering to bereaved families and individuals, that no two people are alike when it comes to dealing with loss. In verse 35 of the Lazarus story, 'Jesus [also] wept.' It is perfectly normal to feel lost and bereft. You go back to work or pop along to the shops or sit on the bus or drive the car, and no one can ever really understand what you might be going through.

The saying that 'time is a great healer' is true; but some people valiantly learn to bear the wounds of sorrow for the rest of their lives. Continuing on life's pilgrimage after losing someone close is a daily challenge; and Jesus' promise that those who mourn will be comforted would, and still does, resonate.

The Beatitudes show a way to life via the kingdom. They deal with personal failings to live up to the task and the universal experience of loss. Whatever hurdles or struggles we face, whatever loss or failure we experience, being aware of God's promise to us and our sense of reliance on God to put things right is the nub of this second saying of Jesus – however challenging at times it may be to accept.

Hospice care

This Beatitude demands that we pause, even for just a moment, and offer thanks for the hospice movement, which deals with suffering, doubt, death and hope like no other.

Those who run, raise money for and support hospices deserve our prayers and support. Hospices wonderfully combine the notions of mourning and comfort. They are a perfect example of the kingdom in action in terms of a physical 'place' to be alongside and share with our fellow human beings. They can be, in every respect, 'thin' places where the gap between heaven and earth hardly exists.

Surprisingly, for decades now, the hospice movement has been and remains under severe pressure across the United Kingdom. Continued funding streams are no longer assured, and fundraising from voluntary sources has become increasingly complicated. Trustees of hospices in many parts of the UK need to find new ways of telling their stories in the social-media age. Toby Porter, the chief executive of Hospice UK, speaks of the challenges facing hospices in general and the 'devastating cuts that have shrunk the care hospices can provide'. He has also pleaded for fully funded 'palliative care provided by hospices so they can continue delivering the vital care that patients and families rely on'. With an increasing and aging population and a rising demand for palliative care, the approach offered by hospices is much sought after across all sections of society.[1]

I have been privileged to visit various hospices. They can help turn any remaining fear of death upside down in a beautiful way. They are a paradox of being blessed on a journey from life through death to eternity. To be comforted and reassured in the process of dying is an extraordinary blessing. To know of the support given to carers, loved ones and supporters, while bringing a smile through days of many tears, this was and is the kingdom at work.

Do remember often those working in, volunteering for and supporting hospices both in this country and around the world. The prayer that follows is imbued with the feeling of peaceful transition that the hospice movement represents.

Praying

O Lord, support us all the day long of this troublous life, until the shadows lengthen, and the evening comes, and the busy world is hushed, and the fever of life is over, and our work is done. Then, Lord, in Thy mercy, grant us safe lodging, a holy rest, and peace at the last; through Jesus Christ our Lord. Amen. (John Henry Newman, 1801–1890)

---

1 'Nearly Six in Ten Hospices Have Made or Are Considering Frontline Cuts', *Hospice UK*, 18 March 2026, https://www.hospiceuk.org/latest-from-hospice-uk/nearly-six-ten-hospices-have-made-or-are-considering-frontline-cuts, accessed 31.03.2026. See also 'Fair Funding for Hospices', Hospice UK, https://www.hospiceuk.org/fair-funding-hospices, accessed 31.03.2026.

Listening: 'The Lord's My Shepherd'

https://youtu.be/syJFsLZmO8o

This version of Psalm 23 is often sung to the tune 'Crimond' and still evokes hope at times of bereavement. Although there are now many new versions of these words, this is still my favourite.

The hymn ends, like the second Beatitude, by affirming the mercy and goodness of God, which can be experienced through a deepening awareness of our shortcomings, joining the faithful and looking onwards always to eternity.

Goodness and mercy all my life
Shall surely follow me,
And in God's house forever more
My dwelling place shall be.
('The Lord's My Shepherd', Francis Rous, sixteenth century)

Looking

https://collection.ncartmuseum.org/objects/3443/rachel-weeping-for-her-children-jeremiah-3115

Jacob Steinhardt, Rachel Weeping for Her Children *(woodcut, 1916), North Carolina Museum of Art*

A voice is heard in Ramah,
    mourning and great weeping,
Rachel weeping for her children
    and refusing to be comforted,
    because they are no more.
(Jeremiah 31.15)

This depiction of Rachel's sorrow encourages pilgrims to remember the experience of loss and mourning. The artwork speaks of hopelessness and desolation. But, to me, this image is about much more than the physical trauma associated with the loss of an individual or indeed a whole people or nation. It is also about re-enacting the second Beatitude. Here, the struggle is to focus on the God-given, right priorities and how mourning occurs when we continually fall short.

It is to this situation that this Beatitude speaks: hope arrives through the power of the kingdom that Jesus proclaims. We might not always have our priorities right. We strive always to do better and mourn when we know we fail. The onus then is to respond positively.

To repeat the words of my broadcasting colleague Angela Tilby: 'No one who mourns feels "blessed"; but Jesus here surprises us with the extraordinary insight that the mourner is close to the heart of creation, and the depths of grief and disappointment are the seedbed of divine renewal.' Only when this is recognized can the blessing of our now-realized loss be the seedbed of divine renewal.

Questions

1. Which aspects of the story of the raising of Lazarus speak to you most deeply? How do you imagine you might have felt if you had witnessed those events first-hand?
2. What would you say are your top three priorities in life at the moment? How have these priorities taken shape?
3. To what extent does the idea of God's kingdom influence the way you live? How might it become an even greater guiding priority in your daily life?
4. Why do you think the hospice movement has been so successful? And in these challenging times, how can we continue to support and strengthen its vital work?

3

Meekness

Blessed are the meek,
for they will inherit the earth.

> The blessing of the meek gives us a glimpse of how the world could and should be, as well as an anticipation of how it will be when God's purpose for creation is fulfilled – it offers a rich hope to us all.
>
> (Fr Ben Eadon, Priest Administrator of the Shrine of Our Lady of Walsingham)

The word 'meek', the chief focus of Jesus' third Beatitude, is not widely used today. The gradual crescendo of Jesus' teaching continues. The first Beatitude focused on humility of the spirit; the second on spiritual awareness; and here, the theme is meekness because, as St Augustine says, 'No one can be meek unless he has mourned for his sins.' The difficulty for us is that the word 'meek' has almost entirely lost its biblical meaning. To modern ears it sounds like weakness; in the Gospels, as we will discover, it is a form of spiritual strength. Meekness is not the absence of power, but power that has been humbled, healed, and placed at God's disposal.

Pope Francis, in his autobiography, *Hope*, published just before his death at Easter 2025, wrote, 'I am a sinner. This is the fairest definition. And it is not just an expression, a dialectical contrivance, a literary genre, a theatrical pose. I am like Matthew in a painting by Caravaggio: a sinner to whom the Lord has turned his eyes.' The call to meekness is linked to God's mercy. We need both on the pilgrim path.

Jesus almost certainly spoke to his disciples in his native Aramaic, but he was clearly aware of the Hebrew Scriptures. Mary and Joseph found him, aged only 12, 'in the temple courts, sitting among the teachers, listening to them and asking them questions. Everyone who heard him was amazed at his understanding and his answers' (Luke 2.46–47).

By the time the Gospels were written, a decision had already been made about which Greek word best rendered the Aramaic term Jesus used to describe the 'meek' in the Beatitudes. This same linguistic journey – from spoken Aramaic to Greek, shaped by the backdrop of the Hebrew Scriptures – applies to all of the key theological terms in the Beatitudes and is particularly significant in this case.

Jesus may well have been recalling the words of Psalm 37.11:

But the meek will inherit the land
  and enjoy peace and prosperity.

Here, the Hebrew word is *praus*. It is unlikely that the word is associated with any kind of weakness. Rather, it suggests again a quiet kind of strength that is both self-aware and disciplined.

The same word is used to describe Moses (Numbers 12.3), and Jesus could once more be said to be taking up the mantle of Moses as he now presents a new covenant with its two focused commandments reflecting the kingdom that is at hand. 'You see,' Jesus is saying here, 'the powerful are not as strong as they appear. It is the poor, the sick and those who are struggling who are the blessed here. To be meek does not mean to be weak.' Indeed, Jesus makes clear that the 'earth' will belong to those who least expected to have a say in its future. Later in the same Gospel, Jesus declares that 'the last will be first, and the first will be last' (Matthew 20.16).

This is radical stuff. Imagine how the religious leaders would eventually react to this unorthodox interpretation of Scripture.

Meekness is the chief characteristic of those who not only seek first the kingdom but also put it into action. Disciples of the new covenant – which Jesus is, in fact, inaugurating here – put aside what is wrong and sinful, and open themselves up instead to God's grace. This self-realization is a gift that God wishes to share with all who embrace kingdom values.

We now turn to two key stories in the Gospels that bear witness to this Beatitude in action. Jesus is at the centre of the action in both.

First, the well-known story of Jesus washing his disciples' feet (John 13.1–17). Then, the dramatic entrance of Jesus into Jerusalem that marks the beginning of the last days of his life on earth, as the story of his death and resurrection unfolds (Matthew 21.1–11).

Spend some time reflecting on these two key narratives; ponder how they show meekness and gentle self-realization as we look at them in more detail.

Foot washing

The story of Jesus washing the feet of his disciples is one of the most vivid examples of meekness in action in the Gospel accounts. Despite Peter's protesting that it should be the other way round – the disciples washing Jesus' feet – Jesus replies, 'You do not realize now what I am doing, but later you will understand' (13.7).

This unlikely episode is commemorated during Holy Week on Maundy Thursday in many cathedrals and churches, when a re-enactment of the foot washing is part of the liturgy.

The Royal Maundy Service originally involved the reigning monarch doing exactly as Jesus did – washing the feet of their subjects. This was a dramatic and much celebrated reversal of roles. In more recent times, representatives are chosen from the wider community to be given Maundy purses by the monarch as a sign of gratitude for their service to others.

I have been privileged to attend two such services, both involving the late Queen Elizabeth II. One of them was particularly memorable. I was standing near the west door of Derby

Cathedral as Her Majesty the Queen and Prince Philip arrived. They were standing just a metre away from me, waiting for the fanfare announcing the monarch's arrival to be sounded. Completely out of the blue, the Queen turned to me and asked, 'Can I just check that Prince Philip is reading his lesson from the lectern?' I was staggered. 'Yes, Ma'am,' I responded, even though I was not entirely sure, and as the procession set off I speedily departed down the opposite aisle to check with the chief verger that what I had told the Queen was true! But this special service spoke then, and still does today, of the poignant reversal of roles and reflects Jesus' kingdom values in action.

In a similar way, Pope Francis often visited prisons on Maundy Thursday to wash the feet of inmates. The image of the late Pope stooping to wash their feet, and the light in their faces as he re-enacted Jesus' meekness, was hugely symbolic and powerful. It also reinforced Pope Francis' commitment to the poor.

Showing acts of meekness to others is not about being a do-gooder or scoring points. Whether it be taking time out to contact someone who is lonely, or hospital visiting, or going the extra mile by helping when someone least expects it, there are often ways presented to us to show kingdom love for others in action, even a stranger, through an act of meekness. The blessing then is both ways: to the receiver, yes, but to the giver also.

Contradictions

Jesus' riding into the holy city of Jerusalem on a donkey is a real turn-up for the books. The story reflects the nub of the third Beatitude. Everyone is surprised. No one expected the Messiah to arrive in Jerusalem in quite this way. It also marks the start of a road of no return in the story of Jesus' relationship with the religious authorities. They represent the opposite to the meekness Jesus shows.

The world is full of contradictions. Unexpected things happen. Someone turns up; we visit somewhere that surpasses all expectations. We see or hear something totally surprising. In this case, the crowds are so delighted to see Jesus (he has, by now, achieved a kind of celebrity status) that they pick up palm branches, wave them, and shout 'Hosanna'. Imagine what the social-media apps would have made of the event today.

While the foot washing is the focus of Maundy Thursday services, Jesus' arrival in Jerusalem on a donkey is celebrated on Palm Sunday – the start of Holy Week. It is, for many Christians, one of the happiest moments of the Christian year.

Crosses made of palm branches are blessed and shared among the people. I usually lead this ceremony outdoors; the faithful then walk into church singing 'Hosanna' while holding their palm crosses aloft.

The palm cross is a much loved symbol of contradiction. The kingdom is at hand and yet Jesus faces imminent danger. In our parish, the crosses are distributed to those unable to get to church and in our church school.

Many Christians believe Jesus knew what lay in store for him in a matter of days. A deeper story of suffering and redemption was developing but, at this stage, the crowd were unaware of it. What unfolded before the eyes of those watching – between the entry of Jesus into the city of Jerusalem on a donkey and his public crucifixion on the cross – was part of an ongoing battle between goodness and evil, meekness and enmity.

When I hold up my palm cross, which is next to my computer, I am acutely aware of what Jesus did for me. Palm Sunday represents how things are not always as they appear. The unexpected can happen without any warning. It might not have seemed likely to the crowd or even to the disciples, but new life was just around the corner.

Dealing with life's contradictions is part of what it means to be a Christian today: going on the journey; being prepared for anything; but all the time knowing what Jesus has already achieved through his offer of new life and grace.

The earth

Despite the differing political views that exist, it would seem that this Beatitude is unequivocal in calling for Christians to embrace the earth. We are to do so through an approach based on social responsibility and good stewardship of the planet and all its resources.

My generation has been far from meek in our attitude towards the gift of creation. The controversy around global warming remains one of the enduring news stories of our time despite those that still deny it.

I do feel ashamed of the way my generation has lived without any real thought for the planet. I do not believe this was a conscious decision, but rather a result of ignorance as to the cumulative effects of modern life. It is only more recently that people have woken up to the results of a certain way of living and how we might improve our footprint as citizens of the world.

I was walking with my eight-year-old grandson near Brighton railway station. When we walk, he often comments on litter; but, this time, he stopped short when he saw a rejected half-full plastic bottle of mineral water lying in the middle of the pavement. He backtracked, picked it up and went straight to find a bin. He does it all the time. He refers often to the perils of litter, its effects on the planet and especially the pollution of the seas.

The natural history broadcaster Sir David Attenborough has been prolific in reinforcing both the challenge of and our response to climate change across a range of networks. 'The truth is, the natural world is changing. And we are dependent on that world. It provides our food, water, and air. It is the most precious thing we have, and we need to defend it,' he said at the EU Climate Change Summit in 2018.[1] He went on to comment on the consequences of inaction: 'If we don't take action, the collapse of our civilizations and the extinction of much of the natural world is on the horizon.' Technological developments and mass-manufacturing mean that the earth has paid the price in terms of pollution. Our throwaway society is harvesting the ignorance of decades of decision making without a thought for the consequences.

1 From '10 Best Nature Quotes from Sir David Attenborough', *WWF Australia*, https://wwf.org.au/blogs/10-best-nature-quotes-from-sir-david-attenborough, accessed 31.03.2026.

During a visit to the Pacific, António Guterres, the UN Secretary-General (at the time of writing), warned that the region's island nations faced grave danger from rising sea levels and urged the world to respond to the SOS before it is too late.

If it is indeed the meek that 'shall inherit the earth', what we have here is a radical redefinition of true discipleship, echoing the Hebrew Bible's celebration of creation as a divine gift. We either accept the gift and look after it or we reject it and face the inevitable, devastating consequences. In terms of being plentiful stewards of the earth, this means recognizing our failings, doing whatever we can to protect creation and, especially within Christian communities, practising what we preach.

Fr Ben Eadon underlines how the opposite to damage-inducing human beings dominating the earth is the clear way forward: 'The blessing of the meek gives us a glimpse of how the world could and should be, as well as an anticipation of how it will be when God's purpose for creation is fulfilled – it offers a rich hope to us all.'

Saying sorry

Being aware of our shortcomings and seeking God's forgiveness is an act of meekness. Jesus here suggests that it is the meek, those with inner strength and a desire to get things right, who come to the Lord in a spirit of penitence and faith.

They are the ones who reveal the kingdom in all its fullness. A willingness to admit where we fall short as disciples of Jesus, and a longing to grow in holiness, are essential qualities of the humble and meek.

Saying sorry is at the heart of much Christian worship. Whatever the tradition or form of a service, it is highly likely that those who come to worship will expect to say they are sorry to God for their failings and shortcomings. It is based on much of Jesus' teaching where sinfulness is seen to be getting in the way of the kingdom's being recognized. Acknowledging sinfulness is always a starting point (see John 3.3–5).

In many churches, this is called either an 'act of repentance' or a 'confession'. It might be a written or spontaneous prayer led by the priest or worship leader, asking God to accept a sense of sorrow on behalf of each believer. In many traditions, this is usually followed by the offering of forgiveness: a prayer of absolution, when the minister says, in these or similar words, 'Almighty God, have mercy upon you, pardon and deliver you from all your sins, confirm and strengthen you in all goodness and keep you in life eternal, through Jesus Christ our Lord. Amen.'

Outside of worship, from a very early age, children are taught the importance of saying sorry. 'Say you're sorry. Go on,' is a constant refrain in nursery and primary school classes; children learn the joy of making things right and, at the same time, receiving forgiveness.

What begins in childhood does not necessarily become any easier – as adults well know. Apologizing is often easier said than done. It may, at times, be spontaneous but, in my experience, it rarely is: more often, it requires real effort. It becomes a journey from where we are to where we hope to be.

In terms of relationships with others, this surely starts with those closest to us. It is often hardest among family members with whom we may have fallen out. Yet, the relief that accompanies an apology can be redemptive. I am always moved when people tell me about a rapprochement with a family member following a breakdown in communication and the absence of any reconciliatory bridges in sight. Often, all that is needed to heal the situation is for someone to say sorry. But again, this is not always an easy pathway to follow.

The same applies to conflict in the workplace, which can be complex and difficult to resolve. This is equally true in voluntary organizations – including the Church. While offering an apology is often the best starting point and way forward, it is not always easy to achieve.

Saying sorry and seeking God's forgiveness is an essential aspect of any Christian pilgrimage. Joining with others and seeking absolution is a poignant moment.

If it is indeed the meek who are to inherit the earth, the starting point for that radical self-understanding is to approach God daily in a spirit of repentance and thankfulness. And, as we do so, we trust that he can forgive us our sins and give us an opportunity to refresh and renew our behaviour and relationships with others.

Praying

This verse from Psalm 51 is a request to God to give us clean hearts and a spirit of meekness and wonder. It is a wonderful prayer to keep on your desktop or in your wallet or purse.

> Create in me a pure heart, O God,
> and renew a steadfast spirit within me.
> (Psalm 51.10)

Listening: 'All Glory, Laud and Honour'

https://youtu.be/pHN8UAk6Yow

While re-enacting the triumphant entry of Jesus into Jerusalem, Christians often sing this hymn at the start of the Palm Sunday celebrations. It sums up Jesus' meekness, from crucified Lord to ascended King in heaven.

> To you before your passion
> they sang their hymns of praise;
> to you, now high exalted,
> our melody we raise.
> As you received their praises,
> accept the prayers we bring,
> for you delight in goodness,
> O good and gracious King!
> (St Theodulf of Orléans, c. 750–821.
> Translated by John Mason Neale, 1851)

Looking

https://en.wikipedia.org/wiki/File:Jes%C3%BAs_y_el_centuri%C3%B3n_(El_Veron%C3%A9s).jpg

Paolo Veronese's Christ and the Centurion, *painted around 1571, is housed in the Prado Museum in Madrid.*

This painting is an outstanding example of meekness in action. The artist takes up the theme of Jesus and the centurion (see Matthew 8.5–13); and it is worth reading the story as you ponder the image.

Two contrasting worlds are depicted here. On the left are Jesus and his disciples, in whom the kingdom's values are revealed. In stark contrast, on the right-hand side, are the centurion and his entourage. They depict the corrupt values of the world order – the very opposite of meekness.

So, when Jesus observes the meekness of the centurion, how he has recognized the essence of this Beatitude in action, he is amazed and says to those following him, 'Truly I tell you, I have not found anyone in Israel with such great faith' (Matthew 8.10).

Questions

1. In the context of this Beatitude, how would you explain what Jesus means in a way that feels natural and comfortable for you?
2. When was the last time you did something unexpected to help someone? How did the experience feel? What did you learn from it?
3. Tackling global warming involves far more than sorting our recycling correctly. What additional actions – big or small – could you take to care for the planet?
4. Do you find it difficult to say sorry? Can you think of a person or situation where a simple, sincere apology might transform things – and perhaps make that a prayerful intention?

4

Nourishment

Blessed are those who hunger and thirst after righteousness,
for they will be filled.

> Jesus' promise of blessing is reassuring but also challenging. To hunger and thirst after righteousness is not vaguely to hope for it but requires whole-heartedness and passion.
> (Richard Frith, former Bishop of Hereford)

Jesus moves on to the issue of being hungry and thirsty for spiritual food and affirms that the blessed will be satisfied. As Bishop Richard Frith points out, this is a reassuring promise; but the suggestion is also that this is not going to be easy. One of my teachers at theological college in Durham described righteousness as simply being 'in the right' with God. The opposite was also, he explained, the case. Where there is no righteousness, there exists, instead, the wrath of God.

Matthew here uses the Greek word *dikaiosynē* to explain what Jesus probably said to his disciples in his native Aramaic. If a Christian is hungry and thirsty for righteousness, they are, by nature, not happy with the way things are and desire something better. Jesus says that too many people just sit back and accept what is wrong. What is needed is courage to be advocates of the kingdom – a radical new way of living.

After Jesus' resurrection, when the first apostles set off to far-flung corners of the ancient world in order to preach the gospel, the demands of the Beatitudes spoken by Jesus would have been an essential part of their message. The people they were addressing had heard only snippets of information about Jesus of Nazareth. Stories of the demands he made and the kingdom he outlined must have fascinated them. In the world at the time, the people seemed hungry for something – thirsty for real meaning to life.

Addressing the Church in Rome, St Paul is clear about the impact of the establishment of the Christian faith on freedom, equality, forgiveness and redemption – all of which must have been music to his listeners' ears.

Take some time to reflect on these words from Romans 3.21–26.

> *But now apart from the law the righteousness of God has been made known, to which the Law and the Prophets testify. This righteousness is given through faith in Jesus Christ to all who believe. There is no difference between Jew and Gentile, for all have sinned and fall short of the glory of God, and all are justified freely by his grace through the redemption that came by Christ Jesus. God presented Christ as a sacrifice of atonement, through the shedding of his blood – to be received by faith. He did this to demonstrate his righteousness, because in his forbearance he had left the sins committed beforehand unpunished – he did it to demonstrate his righteousness at the present time, so as to be just and the one who justifies those who have faith in Jesus.*

Paul here describes righteousness not as something we achieve but as something we receive – a gift made possible through Jesus' death and resurrection.

It is faith in Jesus that allows us to see God's righteousness at work. This is in stark contrast to the rigidity of the Law and the Prophets, as represented by everything that had gone before. St Paul points out that since we have all done things the wrong way at times, all are equally at fault in God's eyes. God's sacrifice of his Son is a constant reminder of why faith for a Christian is not in vain, however challenging the living out of faith on a daily basis turns out to be.

To be hungry and thirsty for righteousness is to ask God to provide sustenance to be 'in the right' and not to accept the terrible things we see and hear about all the time. Temptation to fail is everywhere. There may not always be things we can do to bring about the kind of change we might deem necessary for the kingdom to be at hand today – but we can pray, share and talk about the better world we know Jesus intended and, where possible, be radical catalysts for change.

Such spiritual nourishment is given in many ways, and none of it is possible without God's help. Through reading the Scriptures, saying prayers, and sharing in the gift of the sacraments, Christians are fed and strengthened in countless ways. One story – told several times in Scripture – echoes this theme of Jesus feeding us, even before the Eucharist became a central part of Christian spiritual nourishment.

Loaves and fishes

Jesus' use of a small boy's picnic to feed a large number of people is one of the best-known stories in the New Testament. But there are, in fact, at least two main feeding miracles in the Gospels that are often confused or merged together. It is possible that they are different versions of the same story.

Take some time to compare Matthew 14.13–21 (the feeding of the 5,000) with Matthew 15.32–39 (the feeding of the 4,000).

In the first story, Jesus is said to use five loaves and two fish – provided by a boy near Bethsaida – to feed 5,000 men, plus women and children. In the second story, seven loaves and a few small fish provided by the disciples feed 4,000 men, plus women and children in the Gentile territory of the Decapolis. The numbers are large. The hunger is real.

Without Jesus' miraculous powers, the people would have gone hungry. Through his presence, they are satisfied. The connection between these stories and Jesus' later acts in an upper room, during what became his 'Last Supper', developed over a period of time. It is especially in John's later account of the feeding miracle (see 6.1–15) that the overtones of what we would now refer to as the Eucharist are felt, but the connection is certainly hinted across all of the stories.

Of course, as well as addressing the physical hunger of the people Jesus is seen to be meeting the needs of all who hunger and thirst for righteousness at many levels.

Here are three references to the spiritual reality of Jesus as the bread of life (all in John 6) which are worth some reflection.

> *Then Jesus declared, 'I am the bread of life. Whoever comes to me will never go hungry, and whoever believes in me will never be thirsty.' (John 6.35)*
>
> *I am the bread of life. (John 6.48)*
>
> *I am the living bread that came down from heaven. Whoever eats this bread will live forever. This bread is my flesh, which I will give for the life of the world. (John 6.51)*

Along the pilgrim route on the shores of the Sea of Galilee – very close to the Church of the Beatitudes described in Part One – stands the beautiful church of Tabgha. Here, pilgrims encounter one of the most remarkable mosaics discovered in the region (see p. 60). Its presence suggests that somewhere in this vicinity, where the church now stands, the disciples and the crowds once marvelled at the actions of Jesus described above.

The Tabgha mosaics demonstrate how Jesus had compassion on those who were physically hungry, and also how he saw the moment as an opportunity to demonstrate his desire to feed the people's spiritual hunger. The crowd ate and were satisfied.

Christians are sustained in the Eucharist because as pilgrims they are nourished by Christ's life to reflect his life in the world as he journeys with them.

The fourth Beatitude acknowledges that such hunger and thirst for righteousness start with a self-realization of what is needed: not the values of the world but the values of the kingdom that Jesus brings about. The connection between this saying of Jesus and his feeding of the multitudes, plus his giving of the gift of the Eucharist, is profoundly significant. All who share in this earthly banquet are one step closer to embracing the values of the kingdom.

Eucharist

One of the most tangible ways this Beatitude is experienced – indeed, felt – spiritually is in the receiving of Holy Communion. A first encounter with the Eucharist remains a profoundly significant moment in the life of any Christian.

In some traditions, as described when we considered confirmation (see pp. 23–4), this is linked directly to Christian initiation. Once confirmed, a candidate typically begins to share in full Communion with the rest of the Church. The New Testament scholar N. T. Wright says: 'The Eucharist is the sign and seal of his presence in our midst ... we need his transforming life to be our life to transform us for his mission in the world.'[1]

Here is how Matthew explains what happened later in his Gospel. Spend a little time reflecting or meditating on this passage.

> *While they were eating, Jesus took bread, and when he had given thanks, he broke it and gave it to his disciples, saying, 'Take and eat; this is my body.' Then he took a cup, and when*

1 'N. T. Wright on Word and Sacraments: The Eucharist', from a lecture given on 6 January 2007, *Reformed Worship*, https://www.reformedworship.org/resource/nt-wright-word-and-sacraments-eucharist, accessed 02.04.2026.

he had given thanks, he gave it to them, saying, 'Drink from it, all of you. This is my blood of the covenant, which is poured out for many for the forgiveness of sins.' (Matthew 26.26–28)

With his Jewish background, Jesus would have been in no doubt about the significance of the Passover meal. Each year, Jews commemorate God's deliverance of Israel from slavery and the covenant made with his people – a celebration that lies at the very heart of Jewish identity and hope. Yet, without fully realizing it, the disciples now find themselves in the presence of the promised Messiah, who is transforming this meal into a supper of remembrance for something about to take place, though not yet fulfilled. It is dramatic in every sense of the word. The bread becomes Jesus' body and the wine his blood – a mystery the disciples would realize over time only after his suffering, death, resurrection and ascension.

This Last Supper becomes the eucharistic feast, sustaining Christians on their earthly journey. Those who are hungry and thirsty for something other than what the world can offer are to be nourished in a new and exciting way.

The tension between past and future in relation to spiritual hunger is very real. The Eucharist is both a memorial or reminder of the work of Jesus and an expression of Christ present with us in the moment of our communion with him and our sharing in all that he did for us.

I am writing this on the Feast of Corpus Christi, celebrated every year on the Thursday after Trinity Sunday, which falls 60 days after Easter Sunday. This feast recalls those stories of Jesus feeding large numbers of people as the Church celebrates Jesus' actual presence in the symbols of bread and wine that are shared at Communion. Christians are reminded of Jesus' words, 'This is my body' and 'This is my blood', and thus identify with the suffering of Jesus at the Last Supper and the journey from the cross to the empty tomb.

Most Christians would readily admit that they hunger and thirst to be more 'in the right' with God. The Christian pilgrimage through each stage of life calls for continual prayer, learning and sharing with others.

In this sense, the Eucharist is one of the central ways in which our hunger for righteousness is truly satisfied.

To hold out our hands to receive the bread, and then share the cup of Jesus' Passion, is to participate fully in the life of the kingdom already present on earth. In a world marked by uncertainty and suffering, the act of receiving Holy Communion remains a constant and immeasurable blessing.

All-age learning

There is a well-known quote by C. S. Lewis: 'You are never too old to set another goal or to dream a new dream.' Learning this lesson at every stage of life is both encouraging and life-changing from a Christian point of view: the call is to open our minds, hearts and souls to the bounty of God's grace in the hope of being satisfied through faith.

Indeed, this Beatitude has always reminded me of our seemingly never-ending search for knowledge. Interestingly, and thanks in no small part to modern technology, the thirst for – and availability of – new ways of learning has grown dramatically, from pub quizzes to online courses and audio learning 'on the move'. As life expectancy increases, there has been a real shift towards learning at every age. We are never too young – or too old – to begin a new course or join a local college or university.

Such a hunger and thirst for knowledge and wisdom can also be a deeply spiritual experience. Many churches regard all-age learning as a key priority. They offer courses such as the Alpha Course or Being With to meet this need. There are many others too, including resources produced for all the seasons of the Church by various denominations.

Our parish study days in Hertfordshire have focused on a wide range of subjects. People of all backgrounds want to know more about various aspects of their faith, whether concerning the Bible, worship, ethics or theology. People might not express it directly in terms of a hunger and thirst to be 'in the right with

God'; but this is surely what it is: a desire to increase knowledge so as to understand the mystery of the things of God in a more profound and exciting way.

Never give up on Bible study as the food that endures during the course of a life's pilgrimage. Drink in the wisdom of those who teach how prayer can bring the kingdom closer each day. Study, as well as engage with, the sacraments of the Church. Such encounters with the divine through wisdom offer strength and sustenance.

Heritage

Closely linked to this desire for knowledge – which nourishes the soul – is a growing interest in heritage and history, something towards which this Beatitude also naturally draws me. As we grow older, our appreciation of the past deepens.

When I studied history, I found it interesting to varying degrees; but now I wish I could return to it all with the perspective I have gained over the years. Recently, I encouraged a group of A-Level history students to absorb the wisdom being offered to them, because it shapes their understanding of the world today. Our thirst for meaning and our hunger to understand life often lead us back to history, where so many of the answers reside.

Every September in the UK and across Europe, days are set aside to remember our heritage. They provide a chance for thousands of people to explore buildings that are usually closed to the public. People wander up bell towers, hang out in little-known libraries and see bits of history that are usually cordoned off.

These special days, when people see well-preserved glimmers of how we used to live, are an opportunity to assess and learn from the past. We are becoming more honest about the way we view our heritage.

A recent British Social Attitudes Survey[2] showed a significant

2 See Sir John Curtice and Alex Scholes, 'British Social Attitudes 41: National Identity – Attitudes and Trends around Conceptions of British Identity', 3 September 2024, *National Centre for Social Research*, https://natcen.ac.uk/publications/british-social-attitudes-41-national-identity, accessed 20.09.2025.

fall in the level of the population's pride in our country's history. This is partly because people are becoming more aware of those parts of history that we now realize were not eras to be proud of or to celebrate. In a 2024 *Guardian* article titled 'Survey Showing UK's Loss of Pride in Its Past Is Encouraging, Says Historian', Professor Alan Lester commented that the results of the survey 'show an awareness that history is complicated, that Britons have done admirable things and deplorable things in the past'. Such a candid approach to recognizing how we have arrived at where we are may not be new, but it is wise.

So, we could define heritage as those traditions, beliefs and values that have fashioned cultural change over many centuries.

One of the joys of engaging with biblical studies has been to understand how learning informs our understanding of faith and belief today. For me, the ancient languages associated with our faith, visits to key archaeological sites, including Qumran (where the Dead Sea Scrolls were discovered), and relating the heritage of sacred texts to our own culture have been fascinating. Many of the original documents on which our faith is based of course span many centuries.

Sacred heritage speaks of the past in the present while looking to the future. But it demands honesty in the process. It puts me in mind once again of St Paul and his letter to the Romans: the past is there to provide wisdom and discernment, encouraging hope and confidence for the future.

Learning is important. History and our heritage teach a great deal. We move into the future with lessons learned from the past and try to do our best in the complex world in which we are called to respond today. Showing a hunger and a thirst to understand who we are is the starting point on the journey towards righteousness and the blessing that Jesus promises.

Praying

Teach me to seek you, and reveal yourself to me as I seek you;
for unless you teach me I cannot seek you,
and unless you reveal yourself I cannot find you.
Let me seek you in desiring you;

let me desire you in seeking you;
let me find you in loving you;
let me love you in finding you.[3]

Listening: 'Alleluya, Sing to Jesus'

https://youtu.be/FTrClYH1Yw4

When I used to play the organ at a church in Hull while still a teenager, I always enjoyed leading with this great Communion hymn – 'Alleluya, Sing to Jesus'. What's more, the third verse sums up this Beatitude perfectly.

Alleluya, Bread of heaven,
  Thou on earth our food, our stay;
Alleluya, here the hungry
  Come to Thee from day to day.
Advocate and Intercessor,
  My Redeemer pleads for me,
On the throne of the Almighty
  Now and to eternity.
(William Chatterton Dix, 1837–1898)

Looking

https://www.bibleplaces.com/wp-content/uploads/2021/01/Tabgha-mosaic-of-fish-and-loaves-tb110106544.jpg

The fifth-century mosaic of loaves and fishes at Tabgha (Church of the Multiplication of the Loaves and Fishes, near Capernaum)

3 From chapter 1 of the Proslogion, *The Prayers and Meditations of Saint Anselm with the Proslogion*, translated by Benedicta Ward (Penguin, 1973).

The fifth-century mosaics at Tabgha, in the Church of the Multiplication of the Loaves and Fishes at the foot of the Mount of Beatitudes, have become famous. Tabgha is traditionally believed to be where Jesus multiplied the loaves and fishes to feed the crowd (Matthew 14.13–21).

The mosaics depict various plants and birds of the region; but the most famous is to be found in the front of the church's main altar and shows two fish, a basket and four loaves of bread. The image has been copied and used on much modern-day artwork and pottery originating from the Galilee area. Viewing it, especially in person but now also online, is a real spectacle. The mosaic is a symbol of how God feeds us through the grace that Jesus repeats in each and every Beatitude.

Questions

1. The stories of Jesus feeding large crowds are among the best-known miracles. How do you imagine the people responded in that moment?
2. Do you find learning new things exciting? What steps have you taken to nurture your thirst for knowledge? Could you be doing even more?
3. Our relationship with heritage and history is continually evolving. How do you find opportunities to engage with the past in meaningful ways?
4. If you attend the Eucharist regularly, take a moment to reflect: how important is this act of worship in the context of your everyday life?

5

Kindness

Blessed are the merciful,
for they will be shown mercy.

> This Beatitude teaches us that the undeserved mercy of God – graciously offered to all through the Paschal mystery of Christ's death, resurrection and ascension – is joyfully received in faith and gloriously revealed in a Christian life of holiness marked by loving works of mercy.
> (Dr David Chapman, Methodist Church District Chair, Bedfordshire, Essex and Hertfordshire District)

Christians are to act with compassion towards others just as God has responded to them. This is movingly portrayed in the fifth tableau of César Franck's large-scale oratorio *Les Béatitudes*. This great piece of music depicts mercy as a powerful spiritual antidote to a world full of venom; it leaves the captive listener in no doubt about the power of sin and the gentle ways of God in offering humanity a way through it.

You might want to pause and listen to Franck's Les Béatitudes *on your chosen streaming platform.*

In what is a mesmerizing and beautiful work, Franck sets each of the eight Beatitudes to music in dramatic style. Orchestra, chorus and soloists combine to highlight the sharp contrast between the sinful ways of the world and God's radical alternative.

St Augustine believed Jesus is here saying that those who treat others with compassion and kindness will be treated by God in the same way. Mercy flows naturally from someone who is aware of their failings and shortcomings.

The Hebrew for 'mercy', used for example in Psalm 136, is *hesed*. It has no direct English equivalent. Think here, rather, of mercy in terms of covenant love, or steadfast loving kindness that endures even in the face of terrible human sinfulness. The prophet Micah answers his own question as to what the Lord requires of the believer. The answer is, 'To act justly and to love mercy (*hesed*) and to walk humbly with your God' (6.8). Mercy flows from God (who is the source) and the believer is encouraged on a daily basis to love this way of living. This is surely how Jesus would have understood the situation based on his time worshipping regularly in the synagogue as a young adult. The love of Jesus' Father is rooted in everything in creation and, as the refrain in Psalm 136 makes clear, it endures for ever.

So, Jesus frames this covenantal and personal understanding of mercy in the context of the good news and the arrival of the kingdom. Later in Matthew's Gospel, Jesus explains that in this new order a believer must show their total commitment to God, whoever their neighbour is (see Matthew 22.37–40). In John's Gospel, Jesus could not be clearer: 'A new command I give you: love one another. As I have loved you, so you must love one another' (John 13.34). This is now the nub of life in the kingdom.

The radical challenge of the fifth Beatitude is to show God's compassion, kindness and understanding to others because God has shown it also to us.

There can be no excuses or compromises, and when things do go wrong – as they inevitably will – confession is required. Saying sorry is an acknowledgement of what we ought to have done in the first place. While the word mercy may not appear often in everyday conversation, its companions – kindness, empathy and love – certainly do. Of these, kindness is perhaps the most familiar and widely valued.

The Kindness Test

This Beatitude inevitably calls to mind those often-unseen acts of kindness. The Merriam-Webster dictionary defines kindness as 'the quality or state of being kind; treating people with kindness and respect' or as 'a kind deed: a favour'. In this respect, kindness reflects a key aspect of showing mercy to others.

More than 160,000 people from 144 countries took part in The Kindness Test, organized by the University of Sussex in partnership with BBC Radio. The resulting radio series, *The Anatomy of Kindness*, highlighted how acts of kindness occur in everyday settings, despite people's hesitation about 'getting involved'. While most acts of kindness come from family or friends, around 9 per cent of respondents said it was a *stranger* who unexpectedly offered help – without any thought for themselves or the possible consequences of their actions.

Looking at the news when presenting the 'Thought for the Day' slot in the *Today* programme on BBC Radio 4, it is surprising to me how many good news stories are still out there despite the constant feed of bad and worrying news. It is reassuring to find news stories that are essentially examples of kindness in action in a variety of ways.

After a random search, I found the story of a stranger who had fixed a busted tyre in a dangerous situation for a vulnerable person; people being kind to residents of a migrant camp; children in Scotland setting up a kindness garden; and gardeners being urged to show kindness to bees during a hot spell. Random but wonderful examples, and it is possible to find them on a daily basis. As the American writer Mark Twain said, 'Kindness is the language which the deaf can hear and the blind can see,' and compassionate kindness often speaks more powerfully than words.

After watching productions over the years of the celebrated musical *Les Misérables*, I began to realize what a fine example Victor Hugo's story is of how small acts can change a life for ever. The kindness of Bishop Myriel, who forgives Jean Valjean and offers him the opportunity to start over again, sets off a chain of redemption that spans the whole story. This type of kindness is often understated. It is offered quietly in the background.

Such acts of kindness are often life-changing for both the giver and the receiver. They carry an inherent spiritual quality and, in the context of this Beatitude, demonstrate how acknowledging God's kindness to humanity becomes the starting point from which kindness can then be shared more widely.

It is not weakness to show people compassion but a sign of strength, as the father shows to the Prodigal Son in one of Jesus' best-known parables (Luke 15.11–32). This, despite the protestations of the other brother who has done nothing wrong. With that in mind, we turn – perhaps inevitably – to the story of the Good Samaritan.

The Good Samaritan

The moral of the parable of the Good Samaritan is timeless and engaging. It is a perfect example of this Beatitude in action. Mercy is given by God, and we have the chance to show it back compassionately to others. But, as this story shows, there are always going to be surprises along the way.

The parable is to be found only in Luke's Gospel and, as such, it fits with the Evangelist's overall message that Jesus is for everyone.

Spend some time reflecting on the story of the Good Samaritan in Luke 10.25–37.

Luke's is the most universal of all the Gospels. He sees a place for all in the kingdom. Jesus tells this story in response to a lawyer who asks what he must do to inherit eternal life. When the conversation turns to 'Who is my neighbour?', Jesus uses the question to set the scene for his parable.

Those listening to Jesus' answer would have understood the deep historical animosity between Samaritans and Jews – thus heightening the surprising way in which the story ends. They might also have known that the 17-mile road between Jerusalem and Jericho was notoriously dangerous and might not have been surprised by the attack that unfolded. Unlike the priest and the Levite, who might both have been expected to help the injured man, it is the Samaritan who steps forward and becomes the equivalent of a modern-day hero.

References to being a 'Good Samaritan' or 'not walking by on the other side' are still often made in media headlines. This suggests that, despite decreased levels of biblical literacy in the wider population, many people still know this story.

One of my former tutors, Professor James Crossley, suggested that, while the parable is used to convey messages of compassion and assistance, its interpretation is also often used by politicians wanting to 'preach' equality and fairness. They would urge their audiences not to 'look the other way' or 'walk by on the other side' without directly alluding to the parable.

It is a story that also captures young hearts and minds and therefore works well in school assemblies. Pupils are usually gripped by the detail. Although many already know the way the story ends, such a lesson in unexpected kindness never fails to challenge the values and expectations of all who hear it.

Jesus then reverses the question and encourages those listening to ask themselves, 'Who then is my neighbour?' He is, of course, asking each person listening the same question today, in a world where there is increasing isolation and fragmentation in many communities.

Jesus' answer is clear. Our neighbour is everyone who needs our love and support regardless of race, creed, colour or gender. The kingdom is not about conforming to religious rules or any kind of legalism. Rather, it is about love in action as the Samaritan unexpectedly reveals. The mercy on show here is loving and practical as well as unexpected. It is an unequivocal call to bring blessings to others by showing mercy in action.

The merciful are blessed because, realizing the mercy they have received from God, they can and do more easily show kindness to others.

Shortly after Luke's account of the Beatitudes, Jesus offers further guidance on how we are to approach and respond to others – especially those we find difficult. This whole section concludes with an unmistakable instruction, the true heart of the Good Samaritan story and this Beatitude: 'Be merciful, just as your Father is merciful' (Luke 6.27–36).

Inclusion

Global citizenship requires a commitment to dialogue and mutual care. Kindness is the moral expression of humility and faith in action.

A key question is whether Jesus' call to show kindness to our neighbour – whoever they may be – truly shapes our lives. This is a challenge, for living with mercy and understanding requires us to reject every form of discrimination. Healthy interfaith relationships demonstrate how diversity of faith can help to build a more unified and wholesome society, fostering mutual understanding. The opposite, of course, is equally true.

Diversity and inclusion have reshaped how many Western societies see themselves with questions of gender identity at the forefront of public debate. For Christians today, this means recognizing every person as their neighbour – worthy of love and support regardless of race, creed, colour or gender. Jesus explains that the kingdom is not about ritual legalism but about love in action.

Over the past half century, the religious landscape of the UK has changed dramatically. One in four people now profess no religion, yet many in that group still pray or practise meditation and mindfulness, often identifying as agnostic rather than atheistic. As the last census confirmed, although non-Christian religious groups remain relatively small, they play a significant role in communities across the country.

Jesus also lived in a region consisting of many different ethnicities and faiths against the backdrop of Roman occupation. I suspect this was in his mind when he told the disciples that the merciful are those who offer understanding and engagement to those whose philosophical or theological framework differs from their own.

An interfaith conference held in Edinburgh in October 2024 reminded delegates that, 'Faith and belief groups have an important role in bringing communities together to foster mutual respect, collaboration and understanding in order to reassure people that difference can be positive.'[1] Interfaith relations in the UK happen at both the national and, more especially, the local level. At times of great national significance or importance, representatives of other faiths are usually represented alongside ecumenical guests (Christians of different denominations). But it is at a local level, in communities where different faiths thrive side by side, that the importance of togetherness and openness is most important.

Antisemitism has risen sharply in many parts of the world over the past decade. In the UK and across Europe, Jewish communities have faced increasing hostility in everyday life. Given the deep ties between Judaism and Christianity, I find this profoundly troubling. When, during Yom Kippur, a special day for observant Jews, an attacker drove into and stabbed worshippers outside the Heaton Park Hebrew Congregation synagogue in Manchester, killing two people and seriously injuring others before being shot dead, the country was rightly shaken. I was staying in the city just two miles away when it happened. In response, political and faith leaders across the UK – and international interfaith bodies – condemned the violence, pledged heightened protection for Jewish communities, and urged solidarity across faiths, underlining the urgent work of interfaith cooperation against antisemitic hate.

---

1 'New Conference Highlights Importance of Interfaith Dialogue', 30 October 2024, *The Church of Scotland*, https://www.churchofscotland.org.uk/news-and-events/news/archive/2024/new-conference-highlights-importance-of-interfaith-dialogue, accessed 04.04.2026.

It is equally worrying that many universities have yet to adopt formal antisemitism statements – a delay that, according to Jewish student groups, allows extremist rhetoric to persist on campuses and reflects the complex dynamics of interfaith relations, institutional priorities and the wider socio-political climate. If the fifth Beatitude is truly to be embraced, there can be no place for antisemitism or any form of racial discrimination.

After the British Labour MP Jo Cox was murdered by a far-right extremist with neo-Nazi sympathies, words from the first speech she made to Parliament were frequently quoted: 'We are far more united and have far more in common with each other than things that divide us.' Loving our neighbour – to overcome hatred in those who would do others harm on the basis of race, gender, religion or anything else – is the starting point of showing mercy by loving our neighbour. Kindness recognizes shared humanity. It is vital for maintaining the moral integrity of pluralistic societies and the dignity of every human being.

Workplace

The fifth Beatitude encourages employers and employees to show compassion and kindness to one another in the workplace. When mercy is offered, it can be returned in abundance – or, at least, it should be.

An overriding theme of the modern era is the pace of change brought about by digitalization, and how this has affected ways in which co-workers and colleagues interact with one another.

Work practices have changed dramatically since the 2020 Covid pandemic. While many still commute daily out of necessity, large numbers now work from home or in hybrid roles. At the same time, the rapid rise of AI is reshaping the job market, with *The Times* reporting a one-third drop in entry-level graduate jobs within six months of the technology's wider adoption. In a 2025 *Times* article titled 'AI Will Leave a Gaping Void for Workaholic World', the journalist James Marriott observed, 'The ability to cultivate a meaningful life outside work may be a defining skill of this new age' – provided the boundary between work and leisure can still be discerned.

The Apple TV+ drama *Severance* is a modern-day parable representing the extremes of how human beings might soon be treated in the workplace. As the story unfolds, workers are programmed to exist in two distinct entities: the personal world and the world of work. The brain is programmed so that one world forgets the other, depending on where the person is, with clear boundaries of time and place. The series spells out the danger of dividing the soul to serve a system. It shows how perilous can be the control that work increasingly has over many.

The welfare of workers and the effects of technology and different ways of working bring how we treat one another at work into sharp focus. It is worth contemplating our priorities in the workplace in the face of tumultuous change. What is important? How do we relate to others at work and at home? How does this affect our faith?

Stress is a hot media topic. Working conditions, expectations and ill-treatment of workers often grab the headlines. The European Trade Union Institute believes that there is an epidemic of psychosocial risks affecting people at work, which results in the deaths of a staggering 10,000 people a year. This number is around two thirds more than those who die from physical accidents because of work.

On the positive side, however, in many places of work, people bear witness to a greater level of understanding. There is an increasing number of policies in place to protect the well-being of the workforce; and, anecdotally, a majority of employers seem to take their responsibilities seriously.

To this extent – and I do witness this a lot in places I visit where people are doing a range of jobs – there is what I would call the quiet power of kindness, which should not be overlooked.

I am thinking, as an example, of a staff team in a primary school. During any task-filled, stressful day, with its targets and predicted outcomes, a word of encouragement or praise (rather than the inevitable criticism) from a headteacher or a parent can go a long way towards boosting confidence and morale. I have often found that kindness at work is rarely about grand gestures.

It is more about a quiet word, a bit of advice, a concern for a family member or someone's well-being – all of which can create an atmosphere of kindness and generosity.

When a workplace culture has the capacity to be positive and kind to its workforce, it has ripple effects. It encourages teamwork and togetherness rather than just competition. It can create a culture of understanding and resilience, especially in tough or challenging times.

People then do not just work harder – they feel safer, more valued, and more willing to contribute their best.

Praying

Lord have mercy *Kyrie eleison*
Lord have mercy ***Kyrie eleison***

Christ have mercy *Christe eleison*
Christ have mercy ***Christe eleison***

Lord have mercy *Kyrie eleison*
Lord have mercy ***Kyrie eleison***

The 'Kyrie Eleison' is a well-known prayer in many Christian traditions. It reflects the nub of the fifth Beatitude. It was one of the very few examples of Greek being used in Latin worship. Those who identify the mercy of God in the actions of Jesus cry out for a share of the mercy God has placed in Jesus' hands (see Mark 10.47 and Matthew 15.22). A believer can pray this prayer daily, asking that the chain of mercy from God through Jesus may allow them to view everyone they meet with love and compassion, whoever they may be.

Listening: the Magnificat

https://www.youtube.com/watch?v=S6fyIKS5s5M

The same Greek word *eleos* is used both by Jesus in this Beatitude and by Mary his mother in what is now called the Magnificat. Mary expresses what Jesus will later reiterate on the Mount of Beatitudes. Those who are humble and who recognize the importance of reflecting God's love in their treatment of others join with Mary in accepting God's purpose to trust without equivocation. Reciting the Magnificat daily is a constant reminder of the call to show God's mercy where we are.

> My soul proclaims the greatness of the Lord,
> my spirit rejoices in God my Saviour;
> he has looked with favour on his lowly servant.
> From this day all generations will call me blessed;
> the Almighty has done great things for me
> and holy is his name.
> He has mercy on those who fear him,
> from generation to generation.
> He has shown strength with his arm
> and has scattered the proud in their conceit,
> Casting down the mighty from their thrones
> and lifting up the lowly.
> He has filled the hungry with good things
> and sent the rich away empty.
> He has come to the aid of his servant Israel,
> to remember his promise of mercy,
> The promise made to our ancestors,
> to Abraham and his children for ever.
> (Luke 1.46–55, *Common Worship*)

Looking

https://www.nationalgallery.org.uk/paintings/jacopo-bassano-the-good-samaritan

Jacopo Bassano, The Good Samaritan, *1562–63, oil on canvas, at the National Gallery, London*

There are many attempts in art to capture the message of Luke's story of the Good Samaritan. Bassano's is a deep reflection of the vibrant storyline. The victim is pictured as almost naked, gaunt and helpless. It is impossible not to see overtones of Jesus' body on the cross. In contrast, the Samaritan is well dressed and has obvious strength as he attempts to lift the badly beaten man on to an animal (Luke 10.34).

Dogs were frequently depicted in such paintings and there are two here. The vague images of the priest and Levite in the dark background serve to heighten the contrast between those who should have known better and the one who was least expected to help. Talking about the importance of faith and doing God's work is one thing; putting it into practice by surprising others, without counting personal cost, is a hallmark of discipleship in the new order of the kingdom.

Questions

1. Why do you think kindness can feel so scarce in many communities today? Is it fear of becoming too involved, a desire for privacy or something deeper?
2. The story of the Good Samaritan remains remarkably powerful. What do you think gives it such enduring relevance?
3. Interfaith relations often face challenges that go beyond polite or symbolic gestures. In practical terms, how might we strengthen them and build genuine understanding?
4. Consider how the modern workplace has changed – and continues to change. What positive developments do you see? How can we protect and uphold people's dignity and integrity within it?

6

Simplicity

Blessed are the pure in heart,
for they will see God.

When I read this beatitude, a priest friend comes to mind who was a renowned preacher and confessor. He was very fond of saying that when we die and appear before our Maker the most important question God will ask of us is: 'In life, did you love extravagantly?' I sincerely believe that those who love appropriately and with liberality during their earthly lives are indeed the pure in heart.

(Canon Daniel Cronin, Catholic parish of Knebworth, Hertfordshire)

Jesus now moves on to the question of purity, whether the disciples have the heart for it and, in the light of how they answer, whether they can truly see God and his purposes for them.

In the kingdom, the blessed are the pure (*katharoi*) in heart (*te kardia*). Remember that, as we have emphasized before, ritual purity was central to Jewish religious life during Jesus' lifetime, with laws from the Torah governing cleanliness, Temple access and daily practices (see Leviticus 11—15). But here Jesus gives the idea of purity a new twist.

St Augustine, a now much valued guide, observes in his commentary on the Sermon on the Mount: 'How foolish then are those who seek to see God with bodily eyes! Purify the eye of the heart by faith, that God may be seen.' This striking image of the 'eye' of the 'heart' leads us naturally to the second part of the Beatitude – 'for they shall see God'.

At this moment, it is really important to recognize how often Jesus was confronted by the various Jewish sects about his attitude to all things legal.[1] So it is not surprising that, later in Matthew, we detect an element of exasperation when Jesus tries to explain his position.

In the light of this Beatitude, spend some time reflecting on this passage:

> *Jesus called the crowd to him and said, 'Listen and understand. What goes into someone's mouth does not defile them, but what comes out of their mouth, that is what defiles them.' Then the disciples came to him and asked, 'Do you know that the Pharisees were offended when they heard this?' He replied, 'Every plant that my heavenly Father has not planted will be pulled up by the roots. Leave them; they are blind guides. If the blind lead the blind, both will fall into a pit.' (Matthew 15.10–14)*

With the arrival of the kingdom, a Christian is called to embrace a new command: to love God and show that love in action, discovering a radical freedom from prescriptive rules. True purity of the soul flows from the heart, because inner purity matters far more than external observance. To be 'pure' in this sense is to be free from spiritual containment by showing devotion and sincerity in all aspects of faith.

And this leads to being able to 'see God' more clearly with a pure heart. People sometimes say that they have 'seen' God in a variety of ways (an act of kindness, a beautiful sunset, during a time of mindfulness); but, in the Hebrew Scriptures, actually seeing God is a rare occurrence. It was usually through dramatic signs, such as a burning bush, a cloud or a voice from heaven. God speaks directly to Moses and makes his position clear: 'You

1 For examples of Jesus being accused of flouting Jewish laws, see Matthew 12.1–8; Mark 3.1–6; Luke 13.10–17; 14.1–6; John 5.1–18; 9.1–16.

cannot see my face, for no one may see me and live' (Exodus 33.20). God is present but still hidden. Even prophets such as Isaiah and Elijah experience God in a variety of unusual ways. The message is consistent: God is holy, powerful, present, but not always fully accessible to human eyes.

On the Mount of Beatitudes, Jesus teaches that those who embrace the call to live out the kingdom in all its fullness will see God in a new way. In fact, before the eyes of his listeners, Jesus is already making God visible in fresh and astonishing ways.

The Incarnation is actually the culmination of the events through which Jesus is revealed as the Messiah to an unsuspecting people. With his coming, the faithful behold God through Jesus and are forever guided by the Holy Spirit.

Even in AD 325, those who gathered to form what became the Nicene Creed wrestled with how best to describe the way God is seen by the faithful. The Creed remains a profound testimony to the mystery of God – Father, Son and Holy Spirit – and to the ways in which our purity of heart is deepened through an awareness of his presence with us.

There are many ways in which we experience this today, living our lives against a backdrop of faith. We glimpse God in the mystery of the Trinity as we reflect on how we treat others and as we examine our priorities – an increasingly challenging task for many in the complexity of modern life.

Empathy

When we set aside religious barriers and rules and seek purity of heart, God can be seen in others. Offering and receiving empathy can become a profoundly life-giving experience.

The word 'empathy' started being used just before the First World War as a translation of the German *Einfühlung*, meaning something like 'feeling into the experience of another person'. It suggests *being on the same wavelength as someone spiritually* – sharing their reactions or feelings. It was first used by psychologists to describe the ability to project oneself into the experience of another, especially in relation to art and aesthetics.

A powerful modern parable of empathy unfolds in a BBC documentary, *Field of Dreams*, featuring the former England cricketer Freddie Flintoff. After retiring from professional sport, Freddie became a familiar face on television, until a life-changing accident suddenly halted everything, leaving him with serious injuries and a long road to recovery. Before that tragic event, Freddie had filmed the first series of the documentary – a deeply human story about a group of young men whose lives had been shaped by hardship and limited opportunity. With patience and compassion, he wins their trust, inspires them to believe in themselves, and helps them to form a cricket team – a simple yet profound act of belonging.

Then the devastating crash happens. The boys, hearing of Freddie's injuries, are deeply shaken. What would become of the man who had once believed in them? Months later, after a slow and painful convalescence, Freddie returns to meet them. What follows is profoundly moving: the roles are reversed. The strong has become vulnerable, and those once helped now offer help. Without hesitation, the young men show kindness, encouragement and heartfelt empathy – breathing new strength into the one who first gave them hope.

As well as the social and psychological aspects of empathy, there is also a spiritual dimension that brings us closer to Jesus' teaching in this Beatitude. To be pure in heart, as far as relationships with others are concerned, must involve encouraging mutual understanding in order to be able to see God at work.

The human spirit is affected both by *who* we are and by *what* we feel. Here, the story of the Good Samaritan again comes to mind. But this is much more than a response to action by helping another person practically. In order to see God in others, there is a need to tune in and to be alongside another person. The call is to be calm, to engage spiritually, to see the light of the promise of God's glory into the future. This brings to mind the words of the first letter of Peter: 'Finally, all of you, be like-minded, be sympathetic, love one another, be compassionate and humble' (1 Peter 3.8).

In the end, although the idea of empathy may be relatively modern, it actually represents a profound spiritual relationship between people. Here, Jesus points to the kind of inner clarity that makes true connection possible. To be pure in heart is to meet others without judgement, to listen with openness, and to live with compassion. And in doing so, we glimpse the face of God – not only in heaven, but also in one another.

Detox

There are lots of books and resources about digital detox. Advice on how to reduce screen time is everywhere. But extricating oneself from the digital jungle is easier said than done, as the writer and broadcaster Ruby Wax wrote in a *Times* article, in August 2024, headed 'I Went on a Silent Retreat and Still Had a Nervous Breakdown':

> Social media is a culture where envy is hyped to the limit because instead of seeing what your neighbours are up to, you see globally what people have got that you haven't. When humans are in that state, it brings out the worst.

In this so-called digital jungle, filled with constant noise of various kinds, it is difficult to disconnect and find stillness. Wherever technology is available, the Internet has changed most things about how human beings live their lives. Listening, watching, learning, reading, shopping, and so on: it is increasingly hard to switch off.

But now there is a new and even more worrying challenge that humanity is facing. Artificial Intelligence (AI) is advancing at a dizzying pace, unleashing vast stores of knowledge almost overnight. From graphic design to medical diagnosis, or even finding a recipe or a hotel, answers arrive instantly. It is the sheer speed of technological change that many find unsettling – and which raises deep, practical questions about human life and faith as we continue to look to the future.

In his 2025 autobiography *This Is for Everyone*, Tim Berners-Lee – the inventor of the World Wide Web – laments that the web was once a tolerant, welcoming and slightly anarchic place.

But it can be salvaged yet. His reflection is a reminder that the web, like every human invention, reflects our choices – and still holds the potential to foster connection, empathy and shared purpose rather than division.

In a wonderful series of short articles in his 2025 book *Autocorrect*, the Israeli writer Etgar Keret suggests we are a bit like those grumpy people from *The Muppet Show*, sitting in the stands and making awful noises. The greatest threat that AI poses to our inner sense of purity and well-being is 'not evil robots taking over the world but humans giving in to a homogenising passivity – and by their own volition too'. It is true. We have a choice. What is important is that we keep our heads above water and breathe the pure air of creation without sinking further into the quagmire of meaninglessness. It begins by making sure we always try at least to see things clearly.

Whenever I take a digital detox, which is usually no more than a few hours to be honest, I notice how much better I feel once the pull of devices eases. Apps like TikTok and Instagram can quickly turn dark and negative, so withdrawing, even briefly, can be cleansing. Though the urge to check messages never fully disappears, a short break brings a sense of ease, and people often return to the digital grind feeling refreshed. Even a brief sabbath from the online world can bear real fruit.

In these moments of digital quiet and renewed clarity, we begin to experience what Jesus promised – that the pure in heart, freed from distraction and clutter, shall see God.

A toolkit

In order for us to see God more clearly amid the clutter of daily life, there are some basic steps that often help Christians along the pilgrim way. Some find it easier to read the Bible than to pray. Others go to church but hardly ever study the Scriptures and can find praying quite a challenge. In the quest for a pure heart, this basic toolkit might help.

Bible reading

Although a significant number of Bibles are still sold across the world, many are not widely read. But for those who wish to delve deeper into the wonderful truths of Scripture, to see God more clearly, developing and persisting with regular Bible reading is a great starting point.

Finding the right Bible translation is advisable. Some people find daily Bible reading notes useful. It helps to be acquainted with some of the basic background to any of the biblical books or letters that you choose to read. Switching from one text to another is not that helpful without understanding the context.

Prayer

We have already looked at how big the responsibility is for leading prayers for others in worship. Establishing a regular personal pattern of prayer, reflection and mindfulness in daily life is equally challenging.

This is where modern technology proves a real advantage. There are many apps from a variety of denominations and traditions that might help.[2]

Silence, stillness and making space all add to making prayer time an opportunity to purify the soul.

Joining in worship

The old adage that it is hard to be a Christian on your own is true. Of course, you can 'exist' individually as a Christian but worshipping with others, either in church or in another suitable place, adds a great deal to any pilgrim's quest to see God more clearly. Many shop around to find the church that fits them the

2 My favourites include the following: Church of England Daily Prayer, https://www.churchofengland.org/prayer-and-worship/join-us-service-daily-prayer/todays-prayer; Hallow, https://hallow.com/blog/daily-prayer-prayers-for-today; Pray as You Go, www.prayasyougo.org; all accessed 26.03.2026.

best, which of course is fine. What is important is that you feel 'at home' for worship.

Study

With so many online resources, studying the Bible (as opposed to just reading it) has never been easier. In order to fully embrace the truth of the kingdom as revealed by Jesus, understanding the context of this revelation really helps. There are various times in the Christian year that are identified as moments for personal reflection, re-evaluation and preparation, the most obvious being Advent and Lent. Such seasons give the faithful an opportunity not necessarily to give things up or just to change usual habits, but to take on something extra by focusing on the purity of heart that this Beatitude calls for.

In *I Believe*, a Lent 2025 podcast for the diocese of Chichester, the theologian and spiritual director Dr Robyn Wrigley-Carr encouraged readers to slow down and become more aware of what God is doing in the world. Rather than being swept along by the relentless pace of daily news and demands, she suggests simple, unhurried practices that open us to God's presence: praying a short portion of a psalm each morning, reflecting quietly at the end of the day on where God might have been speaking through events or conversations, and then asking for a deeper awareness of his presence tomorrow.

This is surely what it means to be pure in heart and to live out this Beatitude daily: to have the clarity of vision that comes from slowing down, letting go of distraction and self-preoccupation, and being open to God. In such moments of quiet attentiveness, glimpses of heaven are gleaned as the face of God shines through the ordinary. As St Paul writes to the first Christians at Corinth: 'Let us purify ourselves from everything that contaminates body and spirit, perfecting holiness out of reverence for God' (2 Corinthians 7.1).

Put yourself out there

I have always loved shopping for luggage. The choice of rucksacks now available, for instance, is truly astonishing. Everything – from the old-fashioned, two-strapped shoulder version to the trendier, coloured, over-the-shoulder unisex bag – is widely on sale. Choosing the right one that mirrors your lifestyle and expectations is a big decision.

On my first outing with my newly purchased rucksack, I emptied its contents in my Berlin hotel room only to find a 'note to owner' stitched inside. It simply read, 'Put yourself out there.' This cute message from the person who had finished off my new bag connected directly with me. It did the trick, and it made me smile.

I had been dealing with a few months of health issues and, strangely enough, that message arrived at exactly the moment I needed it. Ever since, whenever I throw that bag over my shoulder, I remind myself: 'Put yourself out there.' It is a daily challenge to be our true selves, and it doesn't necessarily become easier with age. Since the 2020 pandemic, there has been a steady narrative about mental health struggles affecting people of all generations – especially the young.

Added to this are the issues we have just explored – the relentless effects of digitalization, the pressures of the modern workplace, and the shifting nature of personal and family relationships. All of this makes it harder to live with the simplicity and honesty that Jesus calls purity of heart. Yet we need such clarity of being in order truly to see God at work in our lives and in the world around us.

With Jesus' sixth Beatitude in mind, Fr Daniel Cronin (a Catholic priest serving in a parish neighbouring mine in Hertfordshire), reflected on a priest friend. His friend was a renowned preacher and confessor, who was fond of saying that, when we die, God will ask us – perhaps at the very gates of heaven – 'In life, did you love extravagantly?' Fr Daniel went on to suggest that it is those who love freely, generously, and with appropriate liberality during their earthly lives who are truly the pure in heart.

In the end, 'Blessed are the pure in heart' is not about a perfect life or an unblemished record. It is, rather, about living with integrity and openness before God.

It involves detoxing from the distractions and fears that cloud our vision and instead putting ourselves out there in love – even when it feels risky. Such purity is not naïve; it is a deliberate turning away from what is shallow or self-serving, so that our hearts are free to see clearly. Jesus reminds us, 'Where your treasure is, there your heart will be also' (Matthew 6.21).

Praying

Using the Creed as a prayer is a special way of seeing the mystery and intricacies of the way we encounter God. Read it perhaps a line or a section at a time and see how reflecting on the wisdom of those who gathered at the Council of Nicaea still inspires the believer to see God today. In order for our hearts to be pure, we surely want to understand how God reveals himself to us and the wonder of the inter-relationship between Father, Son and Holy Spirit.

> We believe in one God,
> the Father, the Almighty,
> maker of heaven and earth,
> of all that is,
> seen and unseen.
> We believe in one Lord, Jesus Christ,
> the only Son of God,
> eternally begotten of the Father,
> God from God, Light from Light,
> true God from true God,
> begotten, not made,
> of one Being with the Father;
> through him all things were made.
> For us and for our salvation he came down from heaven,
> was incarnate from the Holy Spirit and the Virgin Mary
> and was made man.
> For our sake he was crucified under Pontius Pilate;

he suffered death and was buried.
On the third day he rose again
in accordance with the Scriptures;
he ascended into heaven
and is seated at the right hand of the Father.
He will come again in glory to judge the living and the dead,
and his kingdom will have no end.
We believe in the Holy Spirit,
the Lord, the giver of life,
who proceeds from the Father and the Son,
who with the Father and the Son is worshipped and glorified,
who has spoken through the prophets.
We believe in one holy catholic and apostolic Church.
We acknowledge one baptism for the forgiveness of sins.
We look for the resurrection of the dead,
and the life of the world to come.
Amen.

Listening: 'Blest Are the Pure in Heart'

https://www.youtube.com/watch?v=hpnU2auc3Rk

I love this hymn. I often sing it unprompted when alone in my church, in the car or just walking along. Perhaps that is because it sums up the sixth Beatitude superbly. There are updated inclusive versions of the lyrics, but I prefer the original because of the poetry of John Keble's language. Singing that our hearts may be temples of purity, never doubting what the Lord has promised, whatever hurdles come along, is truly uplifting. Perhaps say it (or sing it) when you have a quiet moment as a prelude to meditation.

Blest are the pure in heart,
for they shall see our God;
the secret of the Lord is theirs,
their soul is Christ's abode.

Lord, we thy presence seek;
may ours this blessing be;
give us a pure and lowly heart,
a temple meet for thee.
(John Keble, 1792–1866)

Looking

https://www.mediastorehouse.co.uk/fine-art-finder/artists/french-school/window-depicting-beatitudes-stained-glass-22308770.html

The Beatitudes in stained glass, L'Huitre Church in L'Aube Department, France

Anyone exploring rural churches in France will know how easy and unexpected it is to stumble across wonderful stained glass. This sixteenth-century renaissance masterpiece is worth a look. The eight panels of the window depict the Beatitudes. I sat in the church to say Evening Prayer and reflected on each of the panels – remembering particularly 'Blest are the pure in heart' as the sun radiated through the glass. It was glorious. Wonderful. I was able to glimpse God in that moment there as the light began to fade and evening came.

Questions

1. Do you think you show love appropriately in your relationships with others? How might this be strengthened or expressed more fully?
2. Empathy comes more naturally to some people than to others. Why is empathy so important in our wider world today?
3. To maintain a healthy balance in your prayer life, what practical steps or habits do you find helpful?
4. 'Be yourself. Put yourself out there.' This was the motto in the rucksack. Is this easier said than done? Why might it feel challenging at times?

7

Peace

Blessed are the peacemakers,
for they will be called children of God.

> 'Peace' can all too readily be described as 'the absence of conflict'. But it's a much greater term than that. Peace encompasses ideas of justice, fairness, beauty, respect, mutual recognition of our common humanity, kindness and much, much more. To be a 'peacemaker' is to be someone who pursues these things, living out to the full the image of God within us that is the extraordinary heritage of every human life. To be a peacemaker is to be blessed as a child of God.
>
> (Michael Beasley, Bishop of Bath and Wells)

Pope Francis returned throughout his papacy to the question of peace in the face of conflict. In *Hope: The Autobiography*, he said: 'Peace is possible. I will never tire of repeating it. It is the fundamental condition for respecting the rights of every human and for the full development of every nation.' The baton for Christians to be agents for peace has already been picked up by his successor Pope Leo XIV whose almost daily utterances continue to urge humanity to make peace our goal.

While Beatitudes 1–6 focus primarily on the inward, spiritual life, the remaining two turn our attention outward – to action, and to putting into practice what God calls those who embrace the kingdom to do. Where there is persecution or victimization, true peace is hard to find. So what, then, is this peace?

The word *shalom* is one of the best known in the Bible and is commonly translated as 'peace'. But in modern-day Hebrew, the word is also a greeting. A Jewish friend of mine once explained that it is not the word *shalom* itself that defines how it should be heard, but the *way* it is said. In every respect, the word suggests harmony, well-being, completeness and, of course, peace.

The Greek word Jesus uses in Matthew, *eirenopoioi*, is usually translated 'peacemakers'. The verb 'to be called', *klethesontai*, is then followed by the theologically charged phrase *huioi theou*. This is variously translated as 'children of God' or, more precisely, as 'sons of God'. So, it is the peacemakers who will be called sons of God. The kingdom exists where peacemakers are gathered.

Without the benefit of hindsight, the early Christians did not at first see a connection between the Passion and resurrection of Jesus and the notion of everlasting peace. Jesus' Passion becomes a parable in itself, linking sin and sacrifice with God's desire for peace through the Incarnation.

The offering of the gift of peace is Jesus' first action in one of his initial resurrection appearances: 'On the evening of that first day of the week, when the disciples were together, with the doors locked for fear of the Jewish leaders, Jesus came and stood among them and said, "Peace be with you!"' (John 20.19). This peace is unlike anything the world can offer. We are not to be troubled or afraid, because the gift of peace is available for us to choose if we so wish.

St John Chrysostom, one of the earliest Church Fathers, believed that accepting and experiencing inner peace is a relevant starting point for any Christian pilgrimage because 'to make peace is to imitate God for He is the God of peace'.

Bishop Michael Beasley, in the quote given at the beginning of this chapter, is clear that peace is not just the absence of conflict. Rather, it takes in justice, fairness, beauty, respect, mutual recognition of our common humanity, kindness and much more. In the light of the cross of Jesus, 'to be a "peacemaker" is to be someone who pursues these things, living out to the full the image of God within us that is the extraordinary heritage of every human life. To be a peacemaker is to be blessed as a child of God.'

Conflict

The news always seems to be dominated by conflict in one place or another. While the war between Russia and Ukraine has filled the headlines throughout the writing of this book, the conflict across the wider Middle East has also been ever-present in the news.

Because the Church of the Beatitudes is situated not far from the Lebanese border, in the north of Israel, I began to contact the sisters who care for the Beatitudes site to check on their well-being.

It was clear that the message of the Beatitudes had been a profound source of comfort to them as they continued their ministry to pilgrims, especially as tensions escalated. In the autumn of 2024, on behalf of my parish, I wrote to assure the sisters of our prayers. Here is the reply from Sr Telesphora Pavlou, which reflects the deep faith and confidence of the community there in the face of much danger:

> Dear Fr Rob
> Thank you so much for your prayer and interest.
>
> Our situation is really very sad ... our life as the life of all people here [near the Mount of Beatitudes] is always at great risk.
>
> From early October [2024] our area, and now in more intensive and expanded way, is under continuous attacks. We remain strong in faith and all sisters remain here; no one else is left.
>
> Triune and One God is protecting us even if we had many fires because of the explosions in the fields around us. Thank God that they succeed to destroy missiles in air, very often on our property ...
>
> We continue praying for peace and for all pilgrims who have been here and for all those who have died. We pray also for those that would wish to come to pray in these holy sites and they are not allowed.

We are sorry for so many innocent people of all areas, nationalities and faiths who are dead in this way or wounded or losing all their houses, etc. ...

Of course we have no pilgrims, no guests in our guesthouse and this creates a great economical problem too as we continue to pay workers, taxes, etc., etc., etc.

Thank you, so much dear Fr Rob! We wait you back with many pilgrims.

In Jesus Christ's love
Sr Telesphora Pavlou and Community of Franciscan Sisters
Mount of the Beatitudes

This letter moved me immensely. Having spent their recent lives and ministries dedicated to a pilgrim site celebrating the kingdom in which peacemakers are to be blessed as children of God, they were now being graphically tested in the most terrible of ways.

Yet, they remained and have remained strong in faith: committed to peace. Recognizing the folly and sinfulness of the world and focusing on God's will is the only way they know. Whatever the threat that each day brings and however frightened they must be, they are witnesses to God's eternal blessing.

To be a child of God is to embrace the kingdom. This kingdom is where the peace of God which passes all understanding reigns supreme. Conflict is what happens when human beings fail to heed the advice offered here. It is tragic; disconcerting; disheartening. But we should never lose faith in the ultimate promise of peace, which is why this Beatitude speaks perhaps most clearly to me today.

Noise

To be a peacemaker in the world is hardly easy. To find peace and quiet is often just as difficult.

In a 2025 *Guardian* article, 'The World Is Getting Noisier, and It's Making Us Ill', the broadcaster Adrian Chiles commented on how difficult he found it to deal with the escalating levels of noise affecting contemporary life: 'the noise, the sheer racket, the crashes, bangs and wallops, the engines, the yelling, the bings and bongs of phone alerts. Oh, we're alert, all right – don't worry about that.' I am sure that many agree with him. And the spiritual impact can be quite dehumanizing.

The one hundredth Archbishop of Canterbury, Michael Ramsey, wrote a beautiful book called *Be Still and Know.* In the context of developing a prayer life that is both contemplative and connected, he writes:

> Silence enables us to be aware of God, to let mind and imagination dwell upon his truth, to let prayer be listening before it is talking, and to discover our own selves in a way that is not always possible when we are making or listening to noise.

It came as quite a shock to realize one morning that I was suddenly deaf in my right ear. When I turned over and put my 'deaf' ear on the pillow I could hear things again with the 'good ear'. Not very well, but I could hear. Long story short, I became the latest in an often-hidden line of people who suffer from what is known as sudden onset sensorial hearing loss. The tinnitus in the empty ear resounds around your brain much of the time, making the sudden deafness even worse. Worse still have been the attacks of vertigo caused by many middle ear problems.

Various social-media support groups proved really helpful. People of all ages and backgrounds daily outlined the same medical journey. The message, as is often the case with these supporting groups, is clear: you are not alone. And the only positive I have experienced since losing my hearing on one side is the ability to turn off the often-constant noise of the world.

With regards to finding peace and quiet more generally in the world, newspapers and magazines have plentiful advice as to how mindfulness and retreats can help. Of course, peace should not only be defined as the absence of noise. In the Bible, peace, as we have already described, is a gift from God. It can become part of our being and personality. If noise distracts, agitates and divides, the peace of God which passes all understanding does the opposite and offers us a road to tranquillity.

In one of the Bible's most famous scenes (1 Kings 19.11–12), Elijah stands on Mount Horeb. He experiences a powerful wind, an earthquake and a fire – yet God is in none of them. Then comes what the King James Version calls 'a still small voice', rendered less effectively by the New International Version as 'a gentle whisper'.

Both phrases, however, capture something essential. The 'still small voice' evokes mystery and poetic quiet; the 'gentle whisper' suggests closeness and tenderness. In a noisy world, both point to the same truth: we meet God in the stillness we must deliberately seek rather than in the clamour of daily life.

Today's children

Jesus refers to the peacemakers as 'children of God' because they bear the family likeness. They reflect their Father's nature when they live out his reconciling love in the world. To receive the kingdom 'like a child' is to accept God's reign not as a negotiated settlement but as a gift – to be embraced with wonder, dependence and a desire for peace.

This childlike state resists the suspicion and competitiveness that often fracture human relationships, making space for the Holy Spirit to create harmony where hostility has been the norm.

This all begs a question that is very close to my heart, as I work closely with many schools in my ministry. What kind of world are today's children growing up in, and what lies ahead for them?

Every year in our parish, we invite Year 6 pupils transferring from one school to another to write down a prayer or a wish on a small card before they leave for senior school. They then place it on the altar and light a candle. Most of them love doing it. It is important to hear their voices. Their vision of peace and purity shines through much of what they write, as does an inherent spirituality – and these young people represent all faiths and none. Here are what a recent group of children offered up on their prayer cards as they lit their candles.

I would like to have kindness in the future. I am grateful to have beautiful siblings.

I hope that my guinea pigs will live long and be healthy.

I would like people that are not as fortunate as me to become more fortunate.

I hope and wish for everyone to have good health and happiness.

Thinking of you, Mum.

I want to be a good/better friend. I want to have real friends. I want my friends to never, ever betray me.

Thank you for this beautiful world you have created.

My only dream is to be a star [with a large picture of a star].

Friends. Memories. Forever.

Jesus says: 'Let the little children come to me, and do not hinder them, for the kingdom of God belongs to such as these. Truly I tell you, anyone who will not receive the kingdom of God like a little child will never enter it.' (Mark 10.14–15). Jesus observes their childlikeness – the openness, trust, and uncluttered vision that children and young people often display while immune to the negativity and problems that many communities in the world are facing.

The prayers and hopes of many young people testify to the fact that such kingdom qualities are still alive and are present in them. Their instinctive longing for kindness, friendship and care for creation naturally reflects God's love. It is the vocation of the Church – and of every follower of Christ – to guard, nurture and learn from these childlike virtues as we grow older.

The kingdom belongs to such as these; sharing their trust and simplicity, we learn what it is to be God's children and inherit not only the promise of peace but the joy of making it real.

Sharing peace

The Church's most visible expression of the seventh Beatitude is the sharing of the Peace during worship.

It is one of the simplest liturgical acts, yet it carries the weight of centuries of Christian tradition. In the Eucharist, just before the altar is prepared for the eucharistic celebration, the celebrant recites a suitable seasonal Bible verse followed by the words of the risen Jesus to his disciples: 'Peace be with you' (John 20.19).

This practice is not a modern invention. The greeting of peace was clearly part of the life of the Early Church. St Paul writes, 'Greet one another with a holy kiss' (Romans 16.16; 1 Corinthians 16.20; 2 Corinthians 13.12), showing that physical and verbal expressions of unity went hand in hand. Paul's point was not about the gesture itself but about what it signified – fellowship in Christ, a visible sign of belonging to one another.

In his *First Apology*, the second-century Christian apologist Justin Martyr describes how believers 'offer prayers for themselves and for all others ... then they salute one another with a kiss'. By about AD 215, the *Apostolic Tradition* – attributed to Hippolytus – gave an explicit instruction: 'Let no one have a quarrel with another; let no one approach the holy mystery with anger. Let us stand in peace with one another before we offer the sacrifice.' This is the heart of the matter.

Before coming to the altar to receive the bread and wine, members of the community are called to lay aside divisions, forgive one another, and stand united in Christ. Whether today's greeting is a kiss, a handshake, a hand wave, or the words, 'The peace of the Lord be with you', it echoes this ancient pattern. This underlines to Christians that worship is not merely a private act of devotion but, especially in the Eucharist, a shared meal of a diverse group of children of God called to bear witness to the peace they are sharing.

For some, the sharing of the Peace can still be surprising, especially for visitors or those unfamiliar with church life. When it was reintroduced more widely, some found it awkward or unnecessary. My late mother used to say, 'I'm glad when that's over with as it's so embarrassing.' But when it is explained and entered into thoughtfully, it becomes far more than a polite exchange. It is a liturgically significant moment in which the truth of the gospel is acted out.

Rowan Williams, the former Archbishop of Canterbury, explains, 'The Peace is not an intermission – it is the Church enacting the truth of what it has heard and believed. Before we share bread and wine, we share forgiveness.' This is why I have made a point of the sharing of the Peace more recently in baptism services, particularly when the congregation is largely made up of those unfamiliar with Christian worship. In that service, I explain this to be an opportunity for the people present to wish one another peace in their lives and in the lives of family and friends in whatever way they choose.

Sharing peace individually with another person – especially after times of stress, disagreement or hardship – is less easy and some never quite achieve it. It is an act that embodies reconciliation. We become children of God by accepting his grace and letting it shape our love for another human being. In doing this, we fulfil the new commandment of Jesus to love one another as he has loved us (John 13.34).

In his commentary on the Sermon on the Mount, St Augustine wrote, 'All the virtues are directed toward the attainment of peace ... and the peacemakers, being perfected in the order of love, are truly God's children.' In the liturgical act of sharing the Peace, this truth is not only proclaimed but enacted.

It is a living reminder that the penultimate Beatitude is not an abstract idea but a calling for the whole Church. We are not passive recipients of peace; we are active participants in God's reconciling work, joined together as his children in love.

Praying

Whenever we are full of anxiety, or even just have anxious thoughts, the words of this verse from Psalm 139 can be a great comfort. As in many of the psalms, the intimacy between God and the believer is key to the faith that is celebrated and proclaimed.

> Search me, God, and know my heart;
> test me and know my anxious thoughts.
> (Psalm 139.23)

Listening: 'Dear Lord and Father of Mankind'

https://www.youtube.com/watch?v=b1MN3chW1Hk

This hymn speaks powerfully of today's quest for peace because it calls for a quieting of the noise that so often affects modern life.

As I wrote in the Introduction, it is a pilgrim favourite when crossing the waters of the Sea of Galilee.

Its imagery of stepping away from turmoil to listen for the 'still, small voice of calm' rings true with many people as they reflect on what may be happening right now in their lives, and it may be the same for you. By reflecting on this Beatitude, we also ask the Holy Spirit to breathe on us and heal us. It is a poem and prayer sung about a timeless path towards peace that feels especially urgent in a fractured, noisy world.

> Breathe through the heats of our desire
> Thy coolness and Thy balm;
> Let sense be dumb, let flesh retire;
> Speak through the earthquake, wind, and fire,
> O still, small voice of calm!
> (John Greenleaf Whittier, 1872)

Looking

https://www.metmuseum.org/art/collection/search/436176

Eugène Delacroix's Christ Asleep during the Tempest, *painted in 1853, is housed in the Metropolitan Museum of Art in New York.*

The contrast between the turbulence of everyday life and the peace Jesus offers is beautifully illustrated in this painting. Any pilgrim taking a boat trip on the Sea of Galilee can easily imagine what it must have been like when the storm engulfed the boat carrying Jesus and his disciples (see Matthew 8.23–27).

The painting portrays a world of torment and tribulation: dark skies, threatening waters, and fear etched on the disciples' faces. Jesus, by contrast, is the embodiment of calm – fast asleep in the stern of the boat. He represents the peace God offers through his blessing as the kingdom is established. Through faith, we too can experience this deep inner peace in a hostile and troubled world.

Questions

1. How do you cope with news of violence and war? How do you reconcile this with God's call for us to be peacemakers?
2. The world is becoming increasingly noisy and distracting. Where do you find moments of genuine peace and quiet?
3. Children often model virtues that adults can lose sight of over time. What examples from children you know have reminded you of these qualities?
4. When did you last share the Peace in a meaningful way? What does this act signify for you when you offer it or receive it?

8

Choices

Blessed are those who are persecuted
because of righteousness,
for theirs is the kingdom of Heaven.

> There's no pain, hatred or injustice that we can endure without our Saviour having been there first. He was persecuted and so he knows both the deep agony of our 'today' and the abundant goodness of our 'tomorrow'.
> (Andy Croft, Associate Rector, St Paul's and St George's, Edinburgh)

The final Beatitude completes the circle. It lands with a surprising weight. Jesus' message is clear. Notice how he ends as he began: by using the present tense. There is no future promise here. The kingdom is already available to those who have recognized it and chosen wisely.

Each previous blessing has revealed a feature of life in God's kingdom: humility, hunger for justice, compassion, a pure heart, the work of peace. However, to live these values out authentically means that, sooner or later, misunderstanding or even hostility can result.

Daily choices have to be made. There are challenges and conundrums throughout our lives. Compromise is not always easy in making judgements and decisions. However laudable are meekness, mercy, purity and peacemaking, the realization that it is far from simple to live these qualities in a world that does not always welcome them is often disconcerting.

The blessing here is offered not in return for a general kind of suffering, but for dealing with opposition or exclusion in the name of righteousness. This Beatitude is about those who endure suffering for a variety of reasons and rarely because of their own actions.

In parish life, I spend a good deal of time listening to wonderful, faithful people talking about the experience of unimaginable suffering. Their humility and faith are natural: they willingly accept suffering or persecution as part of 'taking up their cross and following Jesus'. They rarely demand answers to the most obvious question – 'If I have lived a faithful and relatively good life, why does God allow any of this to happen?' But even if rarely articulated, the question is never far from the surface.

In his commentary on the Beatitudes, St Augustine sees a literary and theological symmetry here. Both the first and the last Beatitude promise the same reward in terms of the kingdom. They bookend the whole journey of the Christian life. By each proclaiming 'for theirs is the kingdom of heaven', they confirm that the journey of discipleship begins and ends with the assurance that God's kingdom is both a present reality and a future hope. Persecution is part of the purifying and proving of the soul. It is not punishment, but a path to glory.

Even in Jesus' day, for any of his followers to survive in such a harsh and challenging context was never going to be easy. To a greater or lesser degree, Christians have faced persecution in every generation; and, in many parts of the world, they still do today. This Beatitude addresses them all.

Jesus also talks here directly to those who are dealing with difficulties, discrimination or any form of individual suffering, including the suffering of loved ones. In the verses that immediately follow, Jesus says:

> Blessed are you when people insult you, persecute you and falsely say all kinds of evil against you because of me. Rejoice and be glad, because great is your reward in heaven, for in the same way they persecuted the prophets who were before you. (Matthew 5.11, 12)

This is a hard but important lesson for anyone embarking on the Christian pilgrimage through life. Jesus looks beyond the present suffering to the reward that awaits in heaven. While the suffering may be challenging at the very least, it will, in the future, be transfigured (see Mark 9.2–8). There can be no glory without sharing in the suffering of Jesus.

The disciples of course would not yet fully understand this. Until the events leading up to Jesus' crucifixion, with the jigsaw as yet incomplete, Jesus often made little sense and seemed to be speaking in riddles. He was quick to point out that they would only understand this at some time in the future. Jesus' example frames the stories of the numerous martyrs whose names the Church commemorates, and the private courage of those known to us who quietly endure difficulty, illness and injustice with steadfast faith in God.

Commemorations

There are examples across the world, often unknown and unreported, of people persecuted for their faith. Among them are a large number of Christians. Their overriding virtue in the face of persecution is courage. In most of the stories told of persecuted Christians, I can only imagine the bravery necessary to face what they endured.

Remembering brave and inspiring people has been a feature of church life for centuries. They are celebrated examples of faith and witness.

Some of those known to us are remembered on certain days of the year. While the *Common Worship* Lectionary used by the Church of England remains a mystery to many (for it can, at times, seem complicated), it is nevertheless an inspirational treasure trove bearing witness to the remarkable faith of individuals and groups of faithful people. A selection of readings from all parts of the Bible is provided for each day, as well as notifications as to who or what should then be remembered.

The Church of England's General Synod have proposed a new commemoration: the Twenty-one Martyrs of Libya. These were 20 Coptic Christians from Egypt and one Christian from Ghana, migrant workers in Libya who, in February 2015, were abducted by the militant group ISIS and executed on a beach near Sirte.

The haunting image of them kneeling in orange jumpsuits, their executioners standing behind them, shocked the world. As they were killed, many whispered the name of Jesus.

Their martyrdom was quickly recognized by the Coptic Orthodox Church, followed by Pope Francis, who included them in the Roman martyrology – an act of ecumenical honour that acknowledged the shared blood of Christian witness. By adding them to its calendar, the Church of England joins in saying: *We will remember them.* Their example is not merely historic. It is a living call to courage, unity and faithfulness in the face of evil.

It is worth remembering here the life and witness of Fr Jerzy Popieluszko, who influenced me profoundly as I was myself ordained priest.[1] Born in Poland in 1947, he was ordained, aged just 25, and soon became the chaplain to the Solidarity movement. Preaching truth in the face of communist oppression, Fr Jerzy spoke of justice, non-violence and the dignity of every person. His homilies were broadcast on Radio Free Europe, inspiring thousands, but also making him a target for the regime.

During the final hours of his life, Fr Jerzy recited the rosary and said:

> In order to defeat evil with good we must take care of the virtue of bravery. It means overcoming your weakness – fear. A Christian should remember that there is only one thing for him to fear – betraying Christ for a couple of pieces of silver. For a Christian it is not enough just to condemn evil, lies, hatred and force. A Christian must himself defend justice, truth and goodness.

In October 1984, four months after I was ordained priest, Jerzy was abducted, tortured and murdered by agents of the Polish secret police. His funeral was attended by hundreds of thousands, and his beatification in 2010 recognized him formally as a martyr. For me, his courage was a revelation. Persecution was not failure – it was the gospel lived without compromise.

1 Fr Jerzy's story has been told by John Moody and Roger Boyes in *The Priest Who Had to Die* (Gollancz, 1986).

I remember calling to mind this eighth Beatitude whenever I thought of him.

Jesus' ministry is framed, as are the first and last Beatitudes, by an understanding that to be courageous in the face of suffering is to share in the knowledge that Jesus has gone ahead of us along the same pathway of rejection and suffering. But none of this suffering is in vain in the light of the kingdom that awaits the faithful. Their courage reverberates. They are examples of faith in action.

Discrimination

Discrimination is rarely out of the headlines. While persecution may take the form of a sustained, often violent, attempt to silence, harm, or destroy someone because of who they are, discrimination is no less damaging. It is often, but not always, subtle. It can take the form of social exclusion, the quiet closing of doors, or the everyday belittling of a person because of who they are. It can be relentless and exhausting for those who experience it.

Being discriminated against can also shape a person's sense of self, narrowing their opportunities and eroding their confidence. Every person bears the image of God – male and female, rich and poor, straight and gay, healthy and sick. Applying this fact to living out the gospel poses questions in today's culture and social backdrop.

St Paul writes to the Galatians, 'In Christ, there is no Jew or Greek, slave or free, male or female' (3.28). This is not merely a spiritual truth to be admired; it is a pattern for Christian living. Jesus' encounters with those deemed different in his own day teach us that dignity is restored not by theory but by relationship – by seeing, hearing and valuing the person in front of us. To treat someone as less than this is to contradict the very heart of the gospel. It erodes their sense of dignity.

Of course, the record of the Church in this regard is questionable. Too often the Church has been, and remains, part of the problem rather than the solution – particularly on questions of gender and sexuality. History is littered with examples of how the

Church has failed to uphold the image of God in every person, sometimes defending cultural prejudice as if it were divine truth. Where we have discriminated, we must repent. Where we have been silent in the face of injustice, we must learn to speak. And where our theology has been used to wound, we must rediscover the Christ who bent down to write in the dust rather than cast the first stone (see also James 2.1–9).

One of the most vivid biblical examples is when Jesus speaks near a well with a Samaritan woman (John 4.5–30). On three clear counts (gender, ethnicity and morality), Jesus turns existing social norms on their head. First, a Jewish rabbi would not normally have addressed a woman in this way in public; then, Jews seemed to have avoided Samaritans as being heretical; and the Samaritan woman's own personal history probably made her an outcast even among her own people.

Yet not only did Jesus speak with her – he offered her living water, restoring her dignity and making her the first in her town to be aware of the reality of what would become known as the kingdom.

As in the case of the third Beatitude concerning meekness and the parable of the Good Samaritan (Luke 10.25–37), we witness similar messages here for Jesus' hearers. He again redefines 'neighbour' as anyone in need, regardless of difference.

To hunger and thirst for righteousness is to long for a world where no one is denied their worth. This longing is not abstract; it must be lived out in how we speak, act and structure our communities. To follow Jesus is to walk towards people the world often avoids, to speak with those it silences, and to make room for the rejected. It is also to embody the truth that the kingdom is a place where dignity is never negotiable, and love is not measured by similarity but compassion.

As well as persecution and discrimination, there is another form of suffering that touches almost every life at some point – the unexpected burdens of illness, frailty and loss. These are not usually the result of hostility or injustice, yet they can feel just as relentless, testing faith to its limits. The Beatitudes speak into this space as well, reminding us that even here, in the midst of weakness, God's blessing can be discovered.

Diagnosis

With this Beatitude in mind, we face a challenging question: how is a person of faith – or indeed anyone – to perceive the kingdom in the midst of suffering for which there is no guilt or responsibility? Illness and frailty often appear from nowhere, unearned and undeserved.

People experience many forms of suffering, including the growing number who serve as carers for loved ones. These are the often-unseen angels within families and communities who have become more visible over the past decade as life expectancy has risen. And as medical research advances and knowledge increases, so too do the stories of complex conditions and illnesses – set against remarkable testimonies of faith, courage and resilience.

I was struck by the neurologist Suzanne O'Sullivan's book *The Age of Diagnosis: Are Medical Labels Doing Us More Harm than Good?* She scrutinizes our cultural rush to label everything. She argues that many diagnoses – though technically correct – do not always benefit patients and may even do them harm. She asks, who is she to criticize those who go straight to 'Dr Google', or indeed AI, to seek an explanation for a rash, an ache, or a strange sensation? The next day it has usually gone, but panic has already set in. Sometimes, it is as simple as the aging process taking its natural course even though we demand explanations. O'Sullivan shares moving patient stories but describes diagnosis as 'the sticking plaster we use to manage life's disappointments'.

In his memorable testimony *Metamorphosis: A Life in Pieces*, Robert Douglas-Fairhurst candidly describes a life-changing diagnosis of aggressive multiple sclerosis. This happened while he was still young, an experience he describes as like falling through a trap door. His body no longer obeyed him. But while his story charts physical decline, it is also a story of personal transfiguration. There *is* a blessing through the diagnosis – a way through it. He turns to the examples of others who have lived with chronic illness and disability. Books become companions, as his suffering deepens, reminding him that he is not alone on his journey.

Hearing such stories conjures up the mighty figure of Job, who, in the Hebrew Scriptures, becomes the archetype of undeserved suffering. The Book of Job explains how he endures wave upon wave of loss and pain – family, livelihood, health. He does not receive easy answers from God. But he does acknowledge God's presence, even in the midst of his suffering. This is the God who speaks out of the whirlwind and the God who, in the end, restores him. Job's cry, 'Though he slay me, yet will I hope in him' (Job 13.15), remains one of the boldest statements of faith in the whole Bible. It is faith forged not in comfort but in calamity.

There is a world of difference between the fleeting anxiety of a symptom search and the crushing weight of a terminal illness, or the daily burden of pain endured over many years. In pastoral ministry, I have often sat with people in these situations, listening to their stories of resilience and sorrow, before having to leave them to endure what I have only glimpsed for a few moments. These encounters are never easy, for they reveal the limits of words and the necessity of presence.

This kind of suffering may not fit neatly into the category of persecution, yet it prompts the same anguished questions about a God of love. Why? Why me? Why now?

Faith in Jesus does not deny the reality of pain, nor does it allow a diagnosis to define a person's identity. Our truest identity lies not in a medical label, but in the image of God in which we are created, and in our baptism. The spiritual danger lies in allowing illness to become the whole story. Faith invites us instead into a mystery, into embodied hope, and into communities where our worth is not measured by ailment; rather, it is gauged by belonging to Christ, who, throughout his earthly ministry, focused on healing of the whole person.

The rhythm of the Beatitudes leads us back to the eighth blessing. Whether suffering arises from persecution, discrimination or an unexpected illness, the call is the same: to endure faithfully, trusting that the kingdom is already present.

Full circle

The Beatitudes have been our guide through the landscapes of the kingdom of God. Step by step, they have shown us that God's blessing rests not where the world expects, but where grace is most needed.

We began with poverty of spirit, the humility to know our dependence on God. We moved through mourning, which opens the heart to comfort; meekness, the strength to live gently; hunger and thirst for righteousness, the passion for God's justice; mercy, the willingness to forgive; purity of heart, the alignment of the inner life with God's will; and peacemaking, the costly work of reconciliation.

Now we have reached the eighth and final blessing: perseverance in the face of difficulty. It is here that the journey comes full circle. The jigsaw is complete. Just as the first Beatitude promises 'for theirs is the kingdom of heaven', so does the last. The Christian life begins and ends with the same assurance – that God's reign is both our present possession and our ultimate hope.

The Beatitudes are not a checklist of separate virtues to be ticked off, but a portrait of a whole life shaped by God. These glorious sayings are not a ladder to climb, but a circle – each blessing flowing into the next, all sustained by the promise of the kingdom.

Living them will not shield us from hardship. In fact, they prepare us to face it. Humility may be misunderstood. Mercy may be exploited. Peacemaking may be resisted. Purity of heart may be mocked. Hunger for righteousness may provoke opposition. And yet, through it all, we are told, 'You are blessed.'

The blessing is not about pleasant circumstances, but about being held within God's care. It is the deep security of knowing that whatever storms break over us, our lives are anchored in Christ.

Every day we choose whether to live in the spirit of the Beatitudes or in the spirit of the age. The spirit of the age prizes self-sufficiency and promotion. The spirit of the Beatitudes calls us to dependence on God, compassion for others, and courage in the face of risk. The two are not compatible – which is why the final Beatitude underlines a cost worth paying, because what is gained is nothing less than life in God's kingdom.

The circle closes where it began: with the kingdom. But closing the circle does not mean the journey is over. Rather, it sends us out again into the world, carrying these blessings into the places where they are most needed.

The words of my friend and fellow priest Andy Croft sum this up perfectly: 'There's no pain, hatred or injustice that we can endure without our Saviour having been there first.' The Beatitudes invite us to see our lives, in joy and in sorrow, as part of the pattern already traced by Christ himself. He knows the agony of our 'today' and the goodness of our 'tomorrow'.

The Lord's Prayer

It is not surprising that the prayer Jesus gives to the disciples, after they have asked him what words to use when they pray, is essentially a prayer for the values of the kingdom to be established on earth as they are already in heaven.

Whenever the Lord's Prayer is offered, the synergy between it and the Beatitudes is mirrored in the words said all over the world, in hundreds of languages, by Christians of every denomination:

Our Father, who art in heaven,
hallowed be thy name;
thy kingdom come;
thy will be done;
on earth as it is in heaven.
Give us this day our daily bread.
And forgive us our trespasses,
as we forgive those who trespass against us.
And lead us not into temptation;
but deliver us from evil.
For thine is the kingdom, the power, and the glory,
for ever and ever. **Amen.**

www.ingramcontent.com/pod-product-compliance
Lightning Source LLC
LaVergne TN
LVHW100922110826
845155LV00036B/51

* 9 7 8 1 7 8 6 2 2 6 3 7 2 *